I.R'95

10.00

D0583741

WITHDRAWN

Parliament under the Tudors

Jennifer Loach

CLARENDON PRESS · OXFORD

Oxford University Press, Walton Street, Oxford OX2 6DP
Oxford New York Toronto
Delhi Bombay Calcutta Madras Karachi
Kuala Lumpur Singapore Hong Kong Tokyo
Nairobi Dar es Salaam Cape Town
Melbourne Auckland Madrid
and associated companies in
Berlin Ibadan

Oxford is a trade mark of Oxford University Press

Published in the United States
by Oxford University Press Inc., New York

British Library Cataloguing in Publication Data
Loach, Jennifer
Parliament under the Tudors.
1. England and Wales. Parliament
I. Titles 328.42
ISBN 0-19-873092-6
ISBN 0-19-873091-8 (Pbk)

Library of Congress Cataloging in Publication Data
Loach, Jennifer.
Parliament under the Tudors / Jennifer Loach.
Includes bibliographical references and index.
1. Great Britain. Parliament—History. 2. Great Britain—
Politics and government—1485-1603. I. Title.
JN521.L63 1991
328.41'072'09—dc20 90—48927
ISBN 0-19-873092-6
ISBN 0-19-873091-8 (Pbk.)

3 5 7 9 10 8 6 4 2

Printed by Interprint, Malta

For Hannah and Oliver Loach

Preface

THIS book is intended as a guide and general introduction for the student of parliament in sixteenth- and early seventeenth-century England. In recent years, the history of parliament has proved to be even more controversial than most other aspects of this period; I have tried here to present my own interpretation, but also to provide references enabling the reader who so wishes to explore these controversies further. The purpose of the book as an introduction explains the absence of references to manuscript sources which are inaccessible to the non-specialist.

Anyone writing on the history of parliament in the sixteenth century depends on the work of those two giants, Sir John Neale and Sir Geoffrey Elton (although perhaps only a historian who is the pupil of neither would dare to juxtapose the two so closely). An enormous debt is also due to those responsible for the sixteenth-century volumes of *The History of Parliament*, edited by Professor S. T. Bindoff and P. W. Hasler, volumes which can always be relied upon to provide information, both useful and esoteric, as well as entertainment. I am personally extremely grateful to David Dean, of Goldsmiths' College, London, who not only allowed me to read and use his unpublished thesis on 'Bills and Acts, 1584–1601', but also provided me with a copy of it.

This study also depends heavily on the relevant Lords and Commons Journals, and on the collections of Sir Simonds D'Ewes, published as *A Compleat Journal* in 1683. For the first part of Elizabeth's reign it also rests on the material edited by T. E. Hartley, *Proceedings in the Parliaments of Elizabeth I*, i. *1558–1581* (Leicester, 1981). I have made extensive use of the constituency information and biographical details in the sixteenth-century volumes published on behalf of the History of Parliament Trust; all spelling of proper names conforms to this usage.

Spelling and punctuation have, generally, been modernized. In giving dates, the Old Style has been retained, but the year is assumed to have begun on 1 January. The dating of statutes is a complicated matter at this period when sessions very frequently begin in the autumn of one year and go on into the spring of the next. I have chosen to follow the contemporary fiction that the whole of a parliamentary session was one day, and that the first: statutes are therefore dated by the opening of the relevant session.

George Bernard, Alastair Parker, Penry Williams, and Barbara Harvey read drafts of the book, and suggested a multitude of improvements; Barbara Harvey was also my guide and friend amongst the quicksands of medieval parliamentary history. Ian Archer, Cliff Davies, Steven Gunn, Joanna Innes, and Paul Slack have contributed pertinent information and difficult questions. My husband, and my children, to whom the book is dedicated, have ensured that my mind was never too narrowly focused on the parliaments of the Tudors.

J.L.

Somerville College, Oxford
March 1990

Contents

Parliaments of the Tudor Period

Some individual sessions are noted for ease of reference.

HENRY VII

1485, 1487, 1489, 1491, 1495, 1497, 1504

HENRY VIII

1510
1512–14 (Feb.–Mar. 1512, Nov.–Dec. 1512, Jan.–Mar. 1514)
1515 (Feb.–Apr. 1515, Nov.–Dec. 1515)
1523
1529–36 (Nov.–Dec. 1529, Jan.–Mar. 1531, Jan.–May 1532, Feb.–
Apr. 1533, Jan.–Mar. 1534, Nov.–Dec. 1534, Feb.–Apr. 1536)
1536 (June–July)
1539–40 (Apr.–June 1539, Apr.–July 1540)
1542–4 (Jan.–Apr. 1542, Jan.–May 1543, Jan.–Mar. 1544)
1545–7 (Nov.–Dec. 1545, Jan. 1547)

EDWARD VI

1547–52 (Nov.–Dec. 1547, Nov. 1548–Mar. 1549, Nov. 1549–Feb.
1550, Jan.–Apr. 1552)
1553 (Mar.)

MARY

1553 (Oct.–Dec.)
1554 (Apr.–May)
1554–5 (Nov. 1554–Jan. 1555)
1555
1558 (Jan.–Mar., Nov.)

ELIZABETH

1559
1563–7 (Jan.–Apr. 1536, Sept. 1566–Jan. 1567)
1571
1572–81 (May–June 1572, Feb.–Mar. 1576, Jan.–Mar. 1581)
1584–5 (Nov. 1584–Mar. 1585)
1586–7 (Oct. 1586–Mar. 1587)
1589
1593
1597–8 (Oct. 1597–Feb. 1598)
1601

I

Introduction

The origins of parliament lay in the monarch's need for counsel
and consent, and the giving and receiving of advice was the main
purpose of a parliament. Edward I's writ of summons to the earl
of Cornwall in 1295 made this clear:

because we wish to have colloquy and to treat with you and with the rest
of the principal men of our kingdom, to provide for remedies against the
dangers which in these days are threatening our whole kingdom . . . we
command you . . . that . . . you be present in person to treat, ordain and
act, together with us and with the prelates, and the rest of the principal
men and the other inhabitants of our kingdom.

For monarchs, parliaments were occasions on which they could
consult a wider range of their subjects than was normally available. Parliaments were not, of course, the only occasions on
which the king could consult his most influential subjects—he
might summon some of his nobles, or a group of merchants, or a
'great council', that is, an assembly of nobles with a sprinkling of
specially invited humbler persons—but parliaments were the
most important of such occasions. This was because many of
the matters on which the king sought advice involved the levying
of taxation, for which the consent of parliament was necessary.

   The principle had been established long before the Tudors that
the king could raise money from his subjects as a whole only with
their consent: a meeting of parliament had from the fourteenth
century been recognized as the means by which that consent was
given. This was the force of Jack Cade's comment in 1450 when,
speaking of a rumour that 'the king should live upon his people,
and that their bodies and goods are [his]', Cade pointed out that
the king could ask for his subjects' goods only through parliament. In 1496 the principle of parliamentary taxation was to be
clearly upheld when a great council made a grant to Henry VII,
but declared that it had 'not a sufficient authority for the levying
thereof', and that a parliament was therefore needed to facilitate
the collection of the grant.

Moreover, the parliament which gave consent had to be a representative one. By 1300 it had been established that magnates acting on their own had not a sufficient mandate to bind the whole realm: for that, the consent of the representatives of the people was necessary. Such representatives, armed with 'plena potestas', that is, full authority, bound the communities which had sent them to the payment of taxation, something which magnates, who bound only themselves, could not do: as Thomas Smith put it much later, 'the consent of the parliament is taken to be every man's consent' because every man 'is intended to be there present, either in person or by procuration and attorneys'. Indeed, from the 1390s taxes came to be granted by the Commons alone, the Lords merely giving their 'assent'. Thus, although the term 'parliament' was occasionally still applied after 1300 to meetings which did not include representatives of the shires and boroughs, such gatherings were not considered adequate for the granting of taxation. Interestingly, when seven members were sequestered—that is, temporarily excluded— from the Commons in 1593, one of the House suggested that some counties might complain about the taxes then granted, since their representatives had not been able to consent to them, nor been 'present at the grant'.

It was for the king to decide when he needed advice and consent. He summoned parliament, prorogued or dissolved it, and decided upon its agenda. The king even determined who should attend parliament, a matter in which a great deal of flexibility existed. The Lower House in the later Middle Ages, for instance, contained—if they cared to turn up—representatives from thirty-seven English counties, together with members from a somewhat fluid group of about ninety boroughs; which boroughs were invited to send representatives seems to have been left to the discretion of the county sheriffs. The monarch had considerable further potential for influence in the Lower House through the creation of new boroughs, and by his control of election procedure. He also decided who should receive a summons to the Upper House. The twenty-one English and Welsh bishops were normally invited, together with about twenty-five abbots from the major monastic houses, but precisely which of the realm's dukes, marquises, earls, and barons would be summoned was a matter for royal discretion.

In the fifteenth century the monarch still frequently attended meetings of parliament in person, and he retained a considerable amount of prerogative discretion: he could, for instance, amend by a belated proviso acts passed in both Houses and assented to by himself. Henry VII personally added a proviso to the money bill of 1497 to exempt the colleges of Oxford and Cambridge, Eton and Winchester, for example, and he added a clause to a 1504 act dealing with escapes from prison. However, neither Richard III nor Henry VII did this as often as had Edward IV, and after 1510 no monarch was to behave in this rather casual way.

By their control of the summons, prorogation, and dissolution of parliament, their arrangement of its agenda, and their initiative in presenting bills, and amending them, monarchs had considerable control over their parliaments. They had particular influence in the Lower House, both through electoral patronage and through their management of the Commons' business by those of their council who had secured seats there. Moreover, in the mid fifteenth century the monarch came to choose the Commons' speaker, whose subsequent election by the House was thus a mere formality. From the reign of Edward IV the speaker was paid a gratuity for his services to the crown, and in 1472 and 1478 a royal servant, William Allington, was elected to the position. He was the first of many. This link with the speaker, and his close association with royal councillors, ensured that the House of Commons, which had gained considerable power in the Lancastrian period, power which it never gave up, could be controlled by the Yorkist and Tudor kings.

It was, then, the monarch who decided that parliament should be summoned. How often did he do this, and why?

The Tudors—and, indeed, the early Stuarts—summoned parliament only rarely, compared with their predecessors. Whereas in the 158 years between 1327 and 1485 only 42 years went past without a meeting of parliament, 43 years were to be without an aseembly of parliament in the 94 years between 1509 and 1603. Moreover, meetings of parliament were being held at less evenly spaced intervals in the sixteenth century than had earlier been the case: in the late medieval period there were only two occasions (1456–9 and 1478–83) when three or more years passed without a meeting, whereas in the first part of

the sixteenth century there were long gaps between meetings—
1504–10, 1515–23, and 1523–9, for example—and there were to
be long gaps again in Elizabeth's reign, such as that between
January 1567 and 1571.

Historians have argued about the significance of this change. It
has led some, like Professor Roskell, to suggest that parliament
was becoming less politically significant than it had been in the
Middle Ages, contrary to the conventional theory that parliament's power was on the increase in the sixteenth century.[1]
Whether parliament was growing or diminishing in importance
during this period is, obviously, an enormously difficult question, to which the remainder of this book will address itself, but it
should first be noted that on closer inspection the figures reveal
that the contrast between the later Middle Ages and the Tudor
period is less marked than Roskell believed. Forty-eight of the
fifty years of Edward III's reign saw a meeting of parliament, for
instance, but things were very different under Henry VI and the
Yorkists: Edward IV summoned only one parliament, lasting
five weeks, in the last five years of his reign, and Henry VII held
only one, lasting nine weeks, during the last twelve years of his.
But in the period 1529–59 there was a meeting of parliament
nearly every year, no interval of much more than two years
between meetings, and two meetings in some years: the second
part of Henry VIII's reign and the reigns of Edward VI and Mary
were thus periods of frequent parliaments, sandwiched between
half-centuries of infrequent parliaments.

Why was this? One explanation is that the 1530s, 1540s, and
1550s were a period of rapid change in the doctrine and structure
of the English church, change authorized by parliament. The
Reformation, and the Catholic revival, produced an increase in
the frequency with which the crown needed to summon parliament. After the 1559 church settlement the monarch at least
believed that the government and teachings of the church were
now fixed, and parliaments were therefore called less frequently.

But, more important, the monarch was not, in any case,
refusing to call parliaments in the face of persistent demands that
he should do so. Sir Thomas Smith's famous question—'what
can a commonwealth desire more, than peace, liberty, quietness,
little taking of base money [and] few parliaments?'—seems to
have found an echo in many contemporary hearts. Indeed, the

monarch apologized if it were found necessary to summon
parliaments closely together. When, in 1536, Henry VIII sent out
writs for a new parliament just after the end of the Reformation
Parliament it was considered proper to explain in an accompany-
ing letter that the meeting really was essential since 'matters of
most high importance' relating to the succession had arisen. In
1572 the queen went so far as to explain that it was perfectly
legitimate for her to summon a meeting despite the fact that
parliament had assembled the previous year since, she said, there
had been a time in the past when parliaments were summoned
annually. Far from trying to conceal the fact that she called
parliaments a little less frequently than her predecessors, Elizabeth
constantly harped on it. In 1593, for instance, the chancellor in his
speech at the opening of parliament explicitly contrasted
Elizabeth, who was 'most loth to call for the assembly of her
people in parliament', doing so 'but rarely and only upon most
just, weighty and great occasions', with her predecessors. Thus,
although Elizabeth did not summon parliament as frequently as
her predecessors had done in the 1530s, 1540s, and 1550s, there is
no reason to believe that her subjects were disquieted by their
monarch's choice. This contemporary lack of enthusiasm for
frequent parliaments perhaps suggests that it is anachronistic to
judge the significance of parliament as an institution by the
frequency or regularity of its meetings.

What considerations prompted Tudor monarchs to summon
parliament? Every meeting was called for specific purposes, and
most for a variety of purposes. These can be grouped into four
categories. A monarch might wish to associate the significant
members of society with a potentially difficult decision, usually
by the device, however artificial, of seeking 'advice'. This function was well set out in a letter written by Sir William Paget to
Protector Somerset in February 1548 arguing that innovation,
particularly in religious matters, should wait until 'the parliament
time', when it could be effected 'with the advice and consent of
the realm, and the learned men'. The monarch might hope,
alternatively, to convey some message to his realm through
parliament. Thirdly, he might wish to implement some new
policy in a manner enforceable in the courts, that is, through
statute. Fourthly, the monarch might be seeking a grant of
taxation.

In the Middle Ages, parliaments had been summoned for a fifth purpose: justice. Parliament was described as 'the king's court and the highest court he has', and its form and procedure reflected this. The judicial functions of parliament, however, were undertaken only by the king and the Lords, the Commons playing no part beyond that, in some cases, of accuser. The Lords could make judgements against individuals charged by the king, the Commons, or private persons with capital crimes or mis- demeanours in a process known as impeachment. They could reverse erroneous judgements made in King's Bench, and decide suits long depending in other courts. They also had the task of trying peers for treason, felony, and misprision of treason and felony: these trials, presided over by a lord high steward, com- missioned by the monarch, were conducted by the House of Lords, if parliament was sitting, or by a body of peers especially summoned by the king, if it was not.

Although most sixteenth-century commentators continued to describe parliament as a court, its judicial functions largely fell into abeyance under the Tudors. There were no impeachments between 1450 and 1621, and although there were a number of spectacular trials of peers in this period, such as that of the earl of Warwick in 1499, the duke of Buckingham in 1521, and the duke of Somerset in 1552, they all took place outside parliamentary sessions in front of a specially convened assembly. In the event, the trial in 1454 of Thomas Courtenay, earl of Devon, was the last to be held actually in parliament. Only five cases of error are recorded as having come from King's Bench between 1514 (when the Lords Journal began) and 1589, and none between 1589 and 1621. Changes in the functioning of other courts, and in particular the development of the new conciliar courts, relieved the Upper Chamber of what had, earlier, been a considerable press of business. All this was to change, however, in the 1620s with 'an exuberant growth' in the judicature of the Upper House.[2]

Examining more closely the four main motives impelling monarchs in the sixteenth century to summon parliament, we find that one of the most frequently mentioned is a desire for advice and support in a political crisis. In 1536, for instance, a circular letter declared that 'matters of most high importance' had occurred, and 'for the preservation of our honour [and] the state

of our succession' they should be 'discussed and determined in
our high court of parliament to be assembled for that purpose'.
Several of Elizabeth's parliaments were specifically asked for
advice—for instance, the parliament of 1586, summoned at the
height of the crisis over Mary, Queen of Scots. In 1593 the
Commons were informed that they had been assembled 'not to
make any new laws, or to spend any time about other matters,
but only to treat and advise of all the good ways and means that
might be invented for the safety of [the queen's] person and
defence of the realm'. Part of this was, of course, mere rhetoric,
and part a mere sugar coating to the bitter pill of taxation, often
requested at the same time; none the less, Tudor monarchs clearly
felt that associating parliament in this way with potentially
dangerous policy was valuable.

If on the one hand the monarch frequently wanted to know
what the influential members of society advised, he also sometimes wanted to convey a message of his own. A meeting of
parliament was an opportunity to speak directly to the men of
weight and influence in the counties, and an occasion for set-piece
explanations of government policy that could be reported back to
the local community. Parliaments at the beginning of a new reign
were frequently used in this way. The first parliament of
Henry VIII's reign, for instance, witnessed an explicit rejection of
some of his father's policies, in particular those that had led to
financial extortion: one act protected landowners who had suffered through the inquisitions of Empson and Dudley, for
example. Similarly, Edward repealed some of his father's more
unpopular measures, such as the act creating the offence of
treason by words, and the 1539 act of proclamations. His elder
sister repealed Edward's treason legislation in her first parliament, and Elizabeth repealed Mary's. Other messages might also
be conveyed through parliament. In 1531, at the height of
Henry VIII's divorce crisis, opinions given by twelve French and
Italian universities on the validity of the king's marriage to
Catherine of Aragon were read out in the House of Commons,
and more than one hundred books written in support of Henry
were exhibited; members were then told by the chancellor that
they should report in their counties what they had seen and heard,
so that 'all men shall openly perceive that the king hath not
attempted this matter of will or pleasure, as some strangers

report, but only for the discharge of his conscience and surety of
the succession of his realm'.

Parliaments were also, of course, summoned in order that the
monarch could implement his policies. For day-to-day matters of
government the king had his council, and the authority he could
exert by means of the privy seal and the signet, but if he wanted to
enforce some new policy on all his subjects through the common
law courts he had to legislate in parliament. By about 1330
statutes had become distinguished from royal ordinances, and by
the end of the fifteenth century judicial opinion had established
that statutes could modify the common law. Even the fifteenth-
century lawyer Sir John Fortescue, who said that an unjust statute
could be disregarded, distinguished between the monarchies of
England and France by the fact that the English king could rule
his people only by such laws 'as they assenten unto'.

However, in 1957 R. W. K. Hinton argued that statute was to
be submerged in the late sixteenth and early seventeenth centuries
by what he called 'unparliamentary government', that is, orders
implemented on the authority of the monarch, or the monarch
and his council alone.[3] Government action sanctioned only by the
signet, the privy seal, and the great seal was on the increase, he
showed, under Elizabeth and the first two Stuarts, a period in
which the number of pages in the statute book being filled
annually was declining. But Hinton's antithesis between parliamentary and unparliamentary government is misleading.
Parliaments could not, nor in the sixteenth century did they
apparently wish to, carry out the executive functions of government. These were the responsibility of the privy council, that is,
of the twelve to forty men chosen by the monarch for that
purpose. The privy council in theory implemented the policy
decided upon by the monarch, although in practice it sometimes
actually made policy. Much of its business was purely adminis-
trative, however, and even trivial—letters to justices of the peace
asking them to do this or that, instructions about the movement
of prisoners from one jail to another, and so on. In the course of
its business it necessarily produced many pieces of paper—grants
of office, enquiries about the price of foodstuffs, warrants for
payment—and the number of pieces of paper increased as
government attempted to regulate more and more areas of
religious, social, and economic life.

The council also produced proclamations, a class of 'unparliamentary' document particularly censured by Mr Hinton, and one we need to consider at length. It is not difficult to understand Hinton's unease, for proclamations, that is, royal commands 'validated by the royal sign manual, issued under a special Chancery writ sealed with the great seal, and publicly proclaimed', very easily look like an alternative to statute, an alternative that was not subject to parliamentary control.[4] Ominously, according to Hinton, the frequency with which proclamations were issued increased dramatically in the course of the sixteenth century from on average (my calculations) under five per annum in the reigns of Henry VII and his son, to over ten per annum thereafter. But once again, if we break down the figures, we find a more complicated picture. The really high averages occurred in the 1540s and 1550s, which were periods of war. (Even the rate at which Henry VIII issued proclamations rose to an average of almost twelve a year in the post-1540 period.) Times of war and of domestic unrest (such as 1549) necessitated speedy action by central government, and proclamations, which could be sent out in a matter of days, were obviously preferable for this purpose to statute.

In the early Tudor period proclamations were generally used 'for the putting the king's subjects and other[s] in more terror and fear'. Their authority does not then seem to have been questioned: indeed, Thomas Cromwell reported in 1531 that he had asked the lord chief justice what powers the king possessed if no relevant statute were available and the lord chief justice had replied that the king with the advice of his council might make proclamations 'for the avoiding of any . . . dangers' and that 'the said proclamations and policies so devised by the king and his council for any such purpose should be of as good effect as any law made by parliament'.

Despite this, Cromwell made an attempt in 1539 to stand proclamations on a firmer base. The subsequent act 'that proclamations made by the king shall be obeyed' may have been successful in soothing contemporary doubts about the precise role and nature of proclamations, but it was repealed in 1547 and much controversy has subsequently arisen about the intentions of the original bill, which was considerably amended in the course of its passage.[5] There has also been much discussion about the

impact of the statute as finally enacted, and the consequences of
its repeal.

Sir Geoffrey Elton has argued that Thomas Cromwell's intention was to ground the authority of proclamations on statute,
thus subjecting 'the prerogative to the sovereignty of king in
parliament'. The late Professor Hurstfield, however, suggested
that the act was part of Cromwell's plan for a royal despotism.
The fact that contemporaries reported 'many liberal words' being
spoken in the debate, and that the popularity-seeking government of Protector Somerset subsequently repealed the measure,
suggest that the original draft did lead at least some men in
parliament—rightly or wrongly—to worry about arbitrary
power. Most historians would now agree that the original bill
had been intended, perhaps with no sinister purpose, to ensure
that proclamations—or at least, a certain category of proclamations—and statutes had equal authority. However, amendments
in the Lords substantially altered the bill, and the final statute,
whilst it grounded firmly on statutory authority those subsequent proclamations that explicitly claimed their authority
from the act, hedged such proclamations round with so many
restrictions that they were rarely used. The act established a
special tribunal consisting mainly of privy councillors that was
intended to deal with offences against proclamations based on its
authority. However, it proved so difficult to collect a quorum
that the act was amended in 1543 to reduce the number required.
There was opposition in the Commons to this bill, and the
measure's duration was finally restricted to the life of Henry
himself. At Edward's accession, Protector Somerset was therefore faced once again with the same unwieldy court that had
originally necessitated the passing of the 1543 act; feeling,
perhaps, that he had nothing to gain by the maintenance of what
seems to have been an unpopular statute, he therefore decided to
repeal it.

The efficacy of proclamations does not appear to have been
affected by the repeal. The first ruling on the validity of proclamations after the repeal of the 1539 act seems to have been in
1556, when a number of judges concluded that 'the king may
make a proclamation . . . quo ad terrorem populi', to put his
subjects in fear of his displeasure and indignation, but not to
impose any forfeiture, fine, or imprisonment (except, of course,

where a proclamation enforced a statute involving such punish-
ments). The judges went on to argue that 'no proclamation in
itself can make a law which was not made before' since proclamations were 'to confirm and ratify a law or statute, and not to
change a law or to make a new law', although they acknowledged
that many precedents 'to the contrary' could be found. Thomas
Egerton, writing in Elizabeth's reign, likewise declared that it
was the view of lawyers that proclamations had validity when
they were 'in supplement or declaration of a law . . . but for
anything that is in alteration or abridgement they have no
power'.

After 1547 statute and proclamation seem to have gone happily
hand in hand. Early Tudor statutes had delegated authority to
proclamations in matters that could not easily be regulated by
parliament, such as price controls, and the whole field of economic legislation came to rest upon this double foundation.
Sometimes statutes authorized control by proclamation, as in the
case of price fixing and wages limitations. Sometimes proclamation was used to clarify or expand statute, as in the seven
proclamations provoked by the 1533 meat prices act. Sometimes
proclamations were used to reconcile the different claims of
various pressure groups which had been overlooked by the
statute-drafters. Sometimes, too, proclamations were used to
suspend a statute in an emergency, or if problems arose over its
implementation: the 1536 act for the true making of woollen
cloth, for instance, caused difficulties and was suspended by
proclamations more or less annually until a new statute of 1542
amended the earlier one.

Only very occasionally did proclamation 'create' law, except
in the special case of control of the coinage, which was univers-
ally recognized as a part of the royal prerogative. Examples of the
rare overstepping of the recognized limitations are Somerset's
action in 1549 over the seizure of rebels' goods, and—rather less
sinister—the proclamations fixing the price of grain of the later
years of Elizabeth. In general, the neglect of recognized constitutional limits occurred only in an emergency, or when the
proclamation was meant to be backed up rapidly by a statute:
thus, the 1580 proclamation against new buildings in London
was intended to be supported by a statute in 1581, but a series of
accidents held it up until 1593. Proclamations were used in the

sixteenth century, therefore, primarily to back up statute, to declare that the monarch wanted a specific statute particularly carefully observed—or, contrariwise, temporarily suspended.

Certainly contemporaries seem to have voiced few anxieties about their use. The only major discussion of the matter after the passing of the 1539 act and its repeal in 1547 was in the course of a debate in 1576 on a bill that would have allowed the monarch to appoint by proclamation the kind of clothing every degree of person within the realm should wear. The main constitutional objection then expressed appears to have been that the bill would have required publication of the proclamation in one place only, and not in every county, as was normal. However, some members did object that 'a proclamation from the prince should take the force of law, which might prove a dangerous precedent in time to come. For tho' we live now in the time of a gracious sovereign', what might happen in the future? The bill did not succeed. Robert Beale in 1592 warned that the council should 'consider well of the matter and look into former precedents' before issuing proclamations, but there was no major outcry about their use until the reign of James. Even then, it appears that the complaints voiced so forcibly in the 1610 petition against proclamations arose out of the tactless way in which James was using them to promulgate policies which had already been rejected by parliament—most notably Scottish union—rather than because the Commons believed that proclamations were of themselves an evil.[6]

Statute and proclamation were not, then, regarded in the sixteenth century as antithetical. The supremacy of statute was never under threat during this period, and monarchs therefore needed to summon parliament if they undertook some major policy.

Finally, we must consider the granting of taxation as a reason for the summoning of parliament. The principle was clearly established by time of the Tudors that the king could raise taxation only after parliament's consent had been given. As we have seen, the great council of 1496, when granting Henry VII £120,000, declared that a full parliament was needed to facilitate its collection. When Henry VIII's chief minister, Cardinal Wolsey, in 1525 demanded 'the amicable grant', a levy of one-sixth of the income and movable goods of laymen, and one-third of the equivalent wealth of the clergy, Kentish priests claimed that they would be utterly destitute 'if the king's grace should now and also in time to come thus by his grace's letters missives, privy seals, or other ways hereafter require aid of the spirituality as often times as it shall please his grace so to do', but they none the less acknowledged their obligation to pay taxes properly granted. Wolsey's attempt to raise money in this unparliamentary way made him, it was claimed, a 'subvertor of the laws and liberties of England.'[7]

Parliamentary control of taxation was, it is true, somewhat limited by the monarch's control of import and export duties. These duties took two forms: customs, that is, permanent impositions on goods leaving or entering a locality, and subsidies. Initially, customs had been imposed by local authorities, but in 1275 Edward I secured recognition of the monarch's right to what came to be known as 'the ancient custom' on wool and hides. (A 'new custom' was imposed on foreign merchants in 1303, and to this was added in 1347 a levy on the export of cloths by denizens.) The royal claim that these revenues belonged to the crown as of right was not contested in the Middle Ages, and even the additional levies in the form of 'impositions' raised from the reign of Mary onwards did not provoke criticism before the reign of James I. The sums which came to the monarch from such levies on trade were, after all, very much smaller at first than those raised by parliamentary taxation—in the reign of Henry VI, for instance, the wool custom was bringing in between £6,000 and £7,000, whereas a single parliamentary grant of a fifteenth and a tenth would bring in between £24,000 and £30,000.

From 1294 temporary grants, or subsidies, were also made by various assemblies of merchants to assist the crown in emergencies. In 1337 Edward III initiated a more elaborate scheme whereby he gave certain merchants a monopoly on the purchase and export of wool in return for a substantial loan, to be repaid by a greatly increased export levy. For two decades dispute raged in parliament over this agreement. The Commons were violently opposed to monopolies, and they also argued that parliament alone had the right to consent to such arrangements. This view prevailed, and was given formal expression in the statute of 1362 which decreed that 'no subsidy or other charge shall be granted on wool by merchants or any others without the consent of parliament'. Parliament had thus become the only representative fiscal body, but it did so at the cost of allowing the wool subsidy to turn into a permanent peacetime tax. Edward III also established, for the maintenance of the fleet, new levies on wool, wool-fells, wine, and general merchandise: these taxes, known as 'tonnage and poundage', although always described as 'for the safeguard and keeping of the sea', were later paid in peacetime as well as war. ('Tonnage' was a levy on wine, 'poundage' an *ad valorem* tax on general merchandise, imposed at varying rates.)

In the late fourteenth century parliament began to make the grant of these levies to the king for life, instead of for only a year or two. The wool subsidy, and tonnage and poundage, were conceded for life to Richard II in 1398, and to Henry V in the euphoric weeks after Agincourt. Henry VI was given a grant for life in 1453, as was Edward IV after only four years on the throne. Richard III received the grant in his first (and only) parliament, and this precedent was followed in Henry VII's first parliament. Henry's son and his grandchildren were also granted these levies for life in their first parliaments, as was James I. On Henry VII's death the Mercers' Company, with some other London merchant communities, tried to argue that they were not obliged to pay such dues between the death of one monarch and the grant being made in parliament to the next. Their argument was unsuccessful: Sir Thomas Seymour, one of the wardens of the Company, noted ruefully that 'the most part of the parliament house standeth by gentlemen, which bear no charge of the said subsidy, and be willing to grant the same'. The constitutional difficulties thus raised were ignored for over a century: not until the reign of Charles I would the crown again encounter any problems over the wool subsidy and tonnage and poundage. The sums involved were considerable, and the making of these grants for life proves that parliament had no clearly formulated intention of controlling the crown through manipulation of the purse-strings.

On the other hand, if parliamentary control of royal spending was weakened by the practice of conceding these levies to the monarch for life, it was not destroyed, as Henry VII's attempts to increase his revenues from non-parliamentary sources testify. Amongst these other sources of revenue were forced loans and benevolences, that is, free gifts offered in place of the military assistance to which the monarch was traditionally entitled. Benevolences had been raised by Richard II and the Lancastrians, but it was Edward IV who began a more systematic exploitation of what was in effect a national levy, and one not subject to parliamentary assent. However, although Richard III in 1484 tried to make political capital out of condemning Edward's benevolences, they were not generally much resented. This was because contemporaries knew very well that there was a difference between benevolences, which had to be solicited of the people 'graciously', and parliamentary grants, which the king might, if need be, raise by force. Benevolences were reminders of the ancient obligation of all able-bodied men to help the king in times of national danger: they could be justified only in terms of military need and their collection could not necessarily be insisted upon. As one of the king's advisers was to point out in 1544, when urging the levying of a benevolence: 'no man shall pay, but such as may spare it, or will be contented to pay it; the common people shall not be grieved'. When Richard Read, a London alderman, refused to pay the benevolence he was sent off to fight (and die) in Scotland: if he would not give money, he had to give his own body.

Another form of extra-parliamentary levy, and one that was to be widely used by the Tudors, was the forced loan, that is, a loan against which security was offered in the form of repayment under the privy seal. Forced loans were mentioned in parliament only when the monarch asked to be released from his promise to repay the loan. In 1529 parliament freed Henry VIII from his obligation to repay the 1522 loan by a bill whose preamble drew attention to the 'inestimable costs, charges and expenses that the king hath sustained in the defence of the realm and of the faith'. Some disquiet was voiced in the Commons, and one London member, John Petyt, went as far as to declare, 'I cannot in my conscience agree and consent that this bill should pass, for I know not my neighbour's estate. They perhaps borrowed to lend the king. But I know my own estate, and therefore I freely and frankly give the king that I lent him.' The bill was none the less passed, but when another of the London members reported back to his Company he informed them that the king, in giving thanks for the grant, had declared that 'unless right urgent causes move

him (which shall be evident to all his . . . subjects) his grace will
never demand penny of them [more] during his life natural'. If
such a promise was made, it was soon broken, for in 1544 another
act released Henry from his obligation to repay the loan raised
two years before. Mary's forced loan of 1557 was not repaid
because of her death—monarchs never regarded themselves as
committed to the financial obligations of their predecessors—but
Elizabeth was very fond of pointing out that her own conduct in
the matter of forced loans was exemplary. In 1593, for example,
one of her courtiers declared in parliament that 'although her
majesty hath borrowed money of her subjects, besides her subsidies, yet hath she repaid it and answered everyone fully'.

The difference between forced loans and benevolences on the
one hand and parliamentary grants on the other was, therefore,
generally recognized, and the wide use made by the Tudors of
forced loans and benevolences should not obscure the fact that if
the crown wished to enforce payment of a levy on all its taxable
subjects, it had to have parliamentary consent.

The main form taken by parliamentary taxation before the
reign of Henry VIII was the fifteenth and the tenth. This was a
levy on annual income from various forms of property, originally raised at a rate of one-tenth in royal demesne and urban areas,
and one-fifteenth elsewhere. Its yield had been fixed in 1334 and
the burden was portioned out territorially; under the Tudors each
grant brought in about £30,000. In Henry VIII's reign a new tax
emerged, called, rather confusingly, the subsidy. The subsidy
was a levy on annual income from any source and, unlike the
fifteenth and tenth, it was levied on individuals at varying rates
ranging from 1s. to 4s. in the pound, the rate being specified in
each grant. The subsidy soon supplanted the older tax as the most
favoured means of raising money: after 1512 no fifteenth and
tenth was ever granted without a subsidy, although subsidies
were sometimes granted without a fifteenth and tenth. However,
as the century progressed, the subsidy assessments, based on
interrogations on oath before locally appointed officials, became
formalized and inaccurate, and this, as we shall see, caused
Elizabeth severe problems.

Since the Tudors were always short of money the desire to
raise taxation became one of the most compelling reasons for a
summoning of parliament. Yet it did not start like that. In the

period 1485–1547, in which there were sixteen parliaments, there were four in which no grant of taxation was made—1485, 1495, 1510, and 1536 (although in 1485 and 1510 grants of tonnage and poundage were made). In three of the remaining twelve parliaments of the period no grant was made during the first session. Thus, no grant was made until the third session of the Reformation Parliament—and, indeed, because the session was suddenly prorogued before all the formalities were complete, no grant was actually levied until after the sixth session. In the parliament of 1539 no grant was made until the second session, and no grant was made until the second session of the parliament of 1542. These parliaments, then—1529, 1539, 1542—were obviously summoned initially for some reason other than money, the need for taxation arising in the course of the parliament rather than before it.

Nearly half of the parliaments called by Henry VII and his son, therefore, were summoned for a reason that was not financial. Indeed, of only three of the parliaments in this period can it be said that they were summoned specifically to grant taxation: the parliament of 1497 needed to ratify the grant made by the great council the previous year, the parliament of 1523 summoned after Wolsey had already dispatched commissioners to raise loans on the security of the taxation it was expected to grant, and the parliament of 1545 which had indeed been postponed because it was thought unwise to have both the subsidy granted by the parliament of 1542 and a new subsidy being collected at the same time.

The picture does not change much in the two reigns after 1547. Taxation was demanded neither in the first session of Edward VI's first parliament nor in the first of Mary's parliaments. Indeed, Mary did not ask for taxation until her fourth parliament. Before 1558, then, taxation, although an important reason for the summoning of a parliament, was not the overwhelming one.

Under Elizabeth, the situation changed. Elizabeth was the first of the Tudors to ask for taxation in the first parliamentary session of a reign, and only one of her parliaments, that of 1572, passed without any grant being made. By the end of her reign Elizabeth was heavily dependent upon grants of taxation. In the 1590s the average annual income from crown land was £100,000 and that from customs £90,000; the queen was, however, receiving on average £144,000 p.a. from parliamentary taxation. The 1590s were, of course, an exceptional period: as Conrad Russell pointed out in *History* for 1976, subsequent monarchs had by contrast little to gain financially from a meeting of parliament—up to 1621, for example, James I received only £40,000 p.a. on average from parliamentary taxation compared with £70,000 p.a. from impositions. But James ruled in a period of peace, and was able to increase his income from customs very substantially by the 1608 Book of Rates. For Elizabeth, parliamentary taxation was essential. At a time when some historians would have us believe that unparliamentary government was growing, the crown was in fact very reliant upon parliament for supply.

Thus, in the second half of the sixteenth century, taxation was a factor of great importance in the decision to summon parliament. It was not the sole factor—the only gathering of the sixteenth century that appears to have been used simply as a means of revenue-raising was that of March 1553—but it was undoubtedly the most compelling.

Of course, the crown tried even then to avoid giving the impression that it cared only about the grant of taxation. It knew that a bad impression would be created, as Sir Ralph Sadler said in 1566, if when members returned home they could report about their doings only that 'we have done nothing but give away your money'. In 1601 the crown servant Robert Cecil was therefore at pains to refute the suggestion made by one member that the subsidy was 'the alpha and omega of this parliament'. In fact, even if a grant of taxation had been the monarch's main purpose in summoning parliament, once it had been assembled the government always found additional tasks for it.

When they decided to summon a parliament, monarchs generally intended to use it for more than one of the purposes we have been considering. Sometimes these purposes can be discovered from the memoranda prepared by the council, and sometimes they, or at least those matters which the monarch was prepared to acknowledge publicly, were outlined by the chancellor in his speech at the opening of parliament. For some parliaments, however, no such evidence exists, and we have to deduce the government's purposes from its subsequent activities. This can be difficult, for once the summons to parliament had been published, the monarch's subjects themselves began to consider the ways in which they could take advantage of a meeting, for many of them, like their ruler, had plans that they wanted implemented through statute. It is therefore not always possible to distinguish for specific pieces of legislation the initiative of the monarch and council from that of private individuals. None the less, it is essential to remember that the initiative for the summoning of parliament was the monarch's, and his alone.

2

Assembly

When the monarch had decided to summon parliament, chancery was instructed to send out the necessary writs. These were of three kinds: writs of election, summons, and assistance.

Writs of summons and assistance were used to assemble the Upper House. Writs of assistance were sent to various legal officials asking for their attendance in the Upper House. They were:

   (i) the two chief justices, the chief baron of the exchequer, and other judges;
  (ii) the master of the rolls;
 (iii) the king's serjeants-at-law;
 (iv) the attorney-general and the solicitor-general; and
  (v) by an act passed in 1539, for the placing of the lords in parliament, the king's secretaries of state.

Although the secretaries of state were thus permitted to sit in the Upper House, they seem to have preferred election to the Commons to responding to the writ of assistance: writs of assistance were therefore, in practice, responsible for the appearance in the House of the legal element alone.

The attorney-general and solicitor-general were perhaps the most important of those summoned by means of writs of assistance, although the solicitor-general in fact sometimes sat in the Lower House. Indeed, the solicitor-general Richard Onslow was elected speaker of the House of Commons in 1566. A debate and a division took place before his election could be confirmed, but it was Onslow himself who asked whether his oath of loyalty to the monarch as solicitor-general was compatible with his position as speaker. Edward Coke also served as solicitor-general and speaker in 1593. However, although exceptions were made in the early seventeenth century for Henry Hobart and Francis Bacon, the attorney-general was not expected to seek election as a member of the Lower House.

The judges and law officers, who sat on the Woolsack, played an important part in the drafting and refining of legislation in the Upper House. Although they had no vote, they frequently served on committees for examining and revising bills, and they carried important messages and bills between the two Houses, and even, in 1547, served on a joint committee. Indeed, in term time the clash of duties for the judges and law officers could lead to delays in the courts.

There were also some legal assistants who sat in the Lords without a writ: these were the masters in chancery, civil lawyers who served a similar, though inferior, role to that of the other lawyers, and the lord chancellor himself. The chancellor sat in the Lords ex officio and without a writ, even if he were a commoner, probably because, as head of chancery, he was reponsible for the issue of writs and could not therefore issue one to himself. The chancellor presided over the Upper House, and acted as its speaker. On the opening day of parliament he made a speech explaining the reasons for its summons, and he also delivered the closing speech of the session. He received all bills presented to the House, ensured that the correct legislative procedures were followed, and generally managed the House and its business.

The judicial element in the Upper House was one of the main reasons why the Lords were more businesslike and efficient in the dispatch of legislation than were the Commons. It was the legal assistants, in M. A. R. Graves's words, who 'provided a professional stiffening to an assembly of amateur legislators'.[1]

These 'amateur legislators' were assembled by means of writs of summons, which were sent individually to spiritual and lay peers. By the end of the fifteenth century it was routine practice to summon to parliament all bishops who were not foreigners or otherwise absentee, as well as abbots and priors from the large monastic houses such as Westminster, Glastonbury, Battle, and Selby. But with the Dissolution of the Monasteries the composition of the spiritual element in the Upper House changed dramatically, for the abbots and priors disappeared. (It is worth noting, however, that the abbot of Westminster and the prior of St John of Jerusalem were again summoned in Mary's reign: Feckenham, the abbot of Westminster, played an active part in Mary's last parliament, and in the first parliament of Elizabeth's reign.) But with these exceptions, abbots and priors disappeared at the Dissolution. The balance between lay and spiritual peers was thereby fundamentally altered. In the fourteenth century the spiritual peers had sometimes been a majority of those summoned to the Lords and in Henry V's reign the number of lay peers receiving a writ of summons dropped to less than fifty. During Henry VII's reign 48 spiritual peers had regularly received a summons to parliament, whereas writs were never sent to more than 43 temporal peers. In the Reformation Parliament 49 spiritual peers—20 bishops (the foreign bishop of Worcester was not summoned) and 29 abbots and priors—received writs of summons compared with 51 temporal ones; at the end of Elizabeth's reign, by contrast, there were only the 26 bishops in the Lords compared with 52 temporal peers. (Henry VIII had created six new bishoprics, of which five survived.)

How significant this change was in practice is difficult to decide. In the Middle Ages abbots, although regularly summoned, rarely actually attended parliament; even bishops were fairly irregular in their attendance before 1529. Thereafter their attendance improved, and prelates became, especially in the 1540s, amongst the most assiduous attenders. The shrinkage in the number of spiritual peers summoned to parliament may therefore have been counterbalanced by their improved attendance.

Nevertheless, after 1539 the third element of the Upper House, the lay peers, became clearly the largest and most important. This was in part due to the development of the concept of a 'parliamentary peerage'. During the early centuries of parliament, as we have seen, it was not believed that a baron summoned to one parliament must necessarily be summoned to others. Indeed, some peers may have attended parliament without a writ at all, perhaps having been invited orally by the monarch. But in the fifteenth century practice became standardized, and by the sixteenth century the holder of a particular title was summoned consistently or not at all. The handful of exceptions can all be accounted for by the youth, extreme old age, mental instability, dire poverty, absence abroad, or imprisonment of the individual concerned.

The crown in the sixteenth century did not, then, any longer exercise control of the Upper Chamber by selecting the peers to whom writs should be sent. It has been argued, however, that although now forced by custom to send writs to a standardized list of the nobility, monarchs were able to exercise control over who turned up by dispatching private instructions to disaffected peers or prelates informing them that their presence was not required. Tunstall, bishop of Durham, was probably dissuaded from attending the third session of the Reformation Parliament, and Chapuys, the imperial ambassador, reported that Lord Darcy and some of the bishops were kept away from parliament in 1534 by this means. Certain bishops were also instructed not to attend the first of Elizabeth's parliaments; however, because the claims of these bishops to their sees was in 1559 a matter of dispute, the parallel is not exact. The practice of ordering dissidents to stay away was uncommon, however. Perhaps bishops or lay peers who were expected to be hostile to government policy found it easier than did others to secure a dispensation from attendance—peers who received a writ were expected to answer it unless they had been excused by the monarch—but in general the crown in this period was concerned with the problem of persuading peers to attend parliament rather than with keeping them away.

Peers who were unable to attend parliament had the privilege of nominating proxies, and the first days of a meeting would be taken up in the House of Lords by the recording of proxies.[2] Sometimes peers seem to have been instructed by a member of the government as to whom they should choose as their proxy: the earl of Shrewsbury was told by William Petre in 1555, for instance, that he should nominate Lord Montagu and the bishop of Ely, which he duly did. Sometimes peers even sent in blank proxy forms for ministers to complete, as did John, Lord Audley, in 1532. Most peers gave their proxies to privy councillors, and bishops always nominated other bishops. However, there is no evidence before 1581 about how, or indeed whether, proxies actually used their votes. Although the question of proxies was to become politically significant in the 1620s, when Buckingham gained control of a large number of proxy votes, their importance in the sixteenth century seems to have lain in their symbolic role as an indication of the association of an absentee peer with what was being done in parliament, and in the prestige they bestowed on the holder, not in any practical advantage that they gave the government. When Stephen Gardiner, bishop of Winchester, died in the middle of the 1555 parliament he held five proxy votes, but the question of what was to happen to these was never discussed. The exercise of their right to nominate a proxy was a privilege that peers took seriously, and one which the government did a certain amount to regulate, but it was not one that had obvious political advantages.

The way in which the monarch could most obviously exercise control over the composition of the House of Lords was, of course, by means of new peerage creations. However, new peers were rarely, if ever, created simply to strengthen the government party in the Upper House. In 1529, for instance, Henry VIII created five new temporal peers. If the need to bolster up his party in the Lords played any part in these elevations they were spectacularly unsuccessful, since two out of the five were to be executed for treason soon after the parliament was dissolved. Of Mary's six peerage creations two were to be of dubious loyalty. Probably such elevations should be regarded as rewards for past service and not as a piece of political management. There is certainly nothing to suggest that peers believed that as a result of their elevation they owed total subservience to the crown.

Besides, monarchs in the sixteenth century were fairly sparing in their creation of new peers. Elizabeth in particular allowed the number of adult lay peers to decline over her reign from 57 to 52. The size of the peerage caused Burghley some concern in 1588, and in 1598 the earl of Essex tried hard to persuade the queen to create new peers, but without success: votes in the Upper House do not seem to have been a consideration with her. James changed this. There were 81 lay peers by 1615. Numbers thereafter soared, rising by 1628 to 126.

The Lower House was summoned by writs of election. These were directed in the main to the county sheriffs, who then arranged for the election of the knights of the shires—two from each of the English counties (excluding Durham, which was not enfranchised until after the Restoration) and, after 1536, one from each of the twelve Welsh counties. The sheriffs also sent their precepts to the enfranchised boroughs in the county, ordering them to proceed to an election. There were, however, a number of boroughs, towns, and cities that were themselves of county status—these were places such as London, York, Exeter, and Southampton—and their writs went directly to their own civic sheriffs. The exceptions to this pattern were the Cinque Ports, where the warden issued the writs, and the duchy of Lancaster boroughs, for which writs were issued directly by the duchy office.

The writs were directed to sheriffs, who informed the relevant authorities in the enfranchised boroughs, and warned the forty-shilling freeholders to attend for the election of the knights of the shire. The election of the shire members took place in the county town on the day of the month on which the county court usually sat. The sheriff would begin the proceedings by explaining the writ, and he or the leading personages present would propose their candidates. All the freeholders present then shouted out the names of the men they preferred. If there were no contest—and it seems that in the vast majority of cases in the sixteenth century there was not—that was the end: the sheriff declared those nominated to be elected and the writ was returned to chancery. If, on the other hand, there were a competition, the sheriff might find himself unable to judge simply by the noise which name had the most support. What was called a 'view' would then be taken: the parties of the various candidates were separated and the sheriff estimated which was the larger. Only if he still could not decide which party had the most support, or if his verdict were challenged, would a counted vote be taken. Then the freeholders would go before the sheriff in turn, declaring their choice.

How many freeholders turned up for an election obviously depended on whether or not the election was contested. The famous Norfolk election case of 1586 produced a crowd of 3,000, and a disputed Yorkshire election in 1597 seems on good evidence to have attracted nearly 6,000 people. Not all those present were entitled to vote, of course: indeed, not all those voting were always qualified to do so—in a contested election at Montgomeryshire in 1588, for instance, where the franchise was 1,600–1,700, a total vote of over 2,000 men was claimed.

All this gave the sheriff considerable opportunity for manœuvre. He might not warn the freeholders in time for them to assemble for the election, he might read the writ out at an unusual time, or he might grossly abuse the voting system. One sheriff who exploited his position to the full was the man conducting the Hampshire election in 1566, who was said to have spent from 11 a.m. to 2 p.m. eating his dinner in the hope that the party to which he was opposed would grow tired and go home before he was forced to count them. But sheriffs were not the only ones behaving badly on such occasions: after the Merioneth election of 1597 a Star Chamber case was brought against two deputy lieutenants of the county claiming that they had gathered with 300

base people . . . unlawfully armed and weaponed with daggers, pistols, mainpikes, Welsh hooks, swords, bucklers, long staves and gauntlets . . . so that many honest persons of good wealth and credit, fearing the election would prove bloody, did thence depart and those that tarried did give their voices in fear and amazement.

However, contested elections for the office of knight of the shire were uncommon. The History of Parliament Trust estimates that 97 per cent of county elections were not contested in the reign of Elizabeth, or at least did not come to a poll.[3] Instead, the pattern of representation was fixed by the gentry of the county. Thus, for instance, the Knollys family took the senior seat in Oxfordshire throughout the reign of Elizabeth, leaving the remaining families to fill the other seat in turn. Usually such arrangements could be made amicably—for example, in 1529 the Grey and Hastings families each chose one knight for the county of Leicester, and as late as 1601 the same axis was operating. Only if there was a contest for power within the county was there a true contest for the county seats; Norfolk after the fall of the fourth duke in 1571 is an example of such a county, for the elections there in 1572, 1586, 1593, 1597, and 1601 were all strongly contested.

By the mid seventeenth century a tradition had emerged about the independence of county electors, a tradition that led conservative reformers to demand an increase in the number of county seats. In fact, although county elections were in general more free of government interference than were borough elections, some considerable efforts had been made in the early sixteenth century to secure the election of knights of the shire particularly well disposed towards the monarch. Thus, it looks as if Thomas Cromwell tried in 1536—without success—to secure the election in Shropshire of Sir George Blount (brother of one of Henry VIII's mistresses), and in 1539 the earl of Southampton urged the forty-shilling freeholders in Surrey to return his own brother and Sir Matthew Browne 'according to the king's pleasure'. In the same year Sir Edmund Knyvet found it impossible to succeed in Norfolk against the government candidate, for Cromwell wrote telling him to 'conform [himself] to the king's will', and reminding him that everyone had a duty to obey the king. The duke of Norfolk apparently settled this election, for he told Cromwell that he had arranged for the return of men 'as I doubt not shall serve his highness according to his pleasure'. Considerable pains were also taken over the Hampshire election in 1539, where the earl of Southampton deferred the election until Cromwell had picked suitable candidates from a 'schedule of the best men of the county'. In 1547 the council urged Sir Thomas Cheyne, sheriff of Kent, to recommend Sir John Baker 'so to those that have the naming of knights of the shire as at the next parliament he may be made knight of the shire of Kent', but Cheyne was too blunt in his approaches and the council had to write again telling him to soothe the ruffled feelings of the freeholders and to assure them that the council 'meant not nor mean to deprive the shire . . . of their liberty of election'. Baker, who was to serve as speaker for the Commons, finally sat for Huntingdonshire. The privy council took great pains with the by-elections of 1552, and in 1553 made a serious effort to secure the election of well-inclined men to Edward VI's second parliament (see below, pp. 92–3). In these endeavours, perhaps the most determined made by any sixteenth-century government, the counties were not neglected. General letters were sent out asking for the return of 'men of gravity and knowledge in their own [counties] and town fit for their understanding to be in such a great council', but directing that specific recommendations by the privy council should always be followed. Sir William Drury and Sir Henry Bedingfield were recommended as knights for Suffolk in such a letter. Both were elected. Sir Richard Cotton, comptroller of the household, was recommended and returned for Hampshire. Letters were also sent to other counties.

After 1553, however, there was probably little government interference in shire elections, and much of what there was concerned a single county, Essex. The privy council register records the dispatch of a letter in 1559 to Sir Thomas Mildmay, sheriff of Essex, about the election of knights of the shire, and in 1563 the council wrote again about the Essex elections, this time to Lord Rich. When Rich did not respond satisfactorily, the council wrote again asking why he 'should not more regard the satisfaction of our reasonable desires than of your particular ones'. In the Essex elections of 1588 the council intervened to secure the return of two deputy lieutenants of the county. Elizabeth herself wrote to prominent individuals in some counties in 1572 asking them to help secure the return of co-operative members, sending to Nicholas Bacon in Norfolk and to Lord Wentworth in Suffolk. There was intervention in Warwickshire and Worcestershire in 1601, but on a fairly tactful basis.

In general, government intervention in shire elections seems to have been rare after the reign of Edward VI. It was presumably this diminution that made possible the growth of a theory of shire independence.

Borough elections varied enormously, since the borough franchise itself varied so much, from the borough of Gatton in Surrey, where the franchise was exercised solely by the lord of the manor, described in the 1545 return as 'burgess and only inhabitant of the borough and town of Gatton', to a city such as Gloucester with a free citizen vote of between four and five hundred. Many boroughs restricted the franchise to the mayor, aldermen, and councillors. Even where the franchise was wider, real power often lay with the council. In Chichester, for example, one member was named by the guild merchant (that is, the mayor, aldermen, and free citizens), and the other by the commoners; in practice the guild nominated the commoners' candidate. (In 1558 the commoners instead chose one of their own number, but he was refused the freedom of the guild and of the city, which was necessary for his election.) When a writ arrived in Exeter for the election of 1588 the borough council met and 'thought and considered what persons shall be most fit to be proposed to the freeholders at the next county day and by them to be chosen'. In 1593 the council in Exeter again decided on whom it thought 'fit men to be citizens and burgesses for this city . . . to be named by the mayor to the citizens'. The mayor was instructed that if the commoners 'like better of any other persons nevertheless they may chose the same whom they like better', but the council's nominees were elected.

Most boroughs were also subject, at least occasionally, to interference from outside. Only a few, such as Worcester, York, and Bristol, avoided it. As we shall see, the monarch himself might take an interest in an election, and the nobility frequently intervened. A number of parliamentary boroughs were manors in the hands of great families: Plympton, for instance, belonged to the Courtenays before their fall, and the Willoughbys owned Orford. Local magnates might also intervene in an election because they held some office in the borough. Thus, in 1584 the earl of Leicester told Andover that, as high steward, 'I make bold heartily to pray you that you would give me the nomination of one of your burgesses.' A great man like the duke of Norfolk had enormous electoral influence. Norfolk could usually put in his clients at Lewes, Shoreham, Bramber, Reigate, Horsham, King's Lynn, Castle Rising, and Great Yarmouth. Similarly, the earl of Bedford could usually nominate to both seats at Tavistock, one at Bridport, one at Melcombe Regis, and another at Weymouth. The earl of Pembroke could nominate to one seat in each of the Wiltshire boroughs of Wilton, Calne, and Devizes. These were the great men. But even a small country gentleman might have one or two seats at his disposal, as Sir Thomas Copley had at Gatton. As a magnate grew in power and influence, so would his parliamentary patronage increase. Thus Robert Dudley, earl of Leicester, accumulated seats until in 1584 he could nominate one member at Poole, another at Southampton, Tamworth, and Denbigh; he often nominated to one seat at Coventry and another at Lichfield.

Why did boroughs allow magnates to nominate their representatives? Obviously, they desired the favour of the great men of the neighbourhood. Thus, the city of Lincoln in January 1553 not only permitted the earl of Rutland to nominate one of its representatives, but also sent him a tun of claret 'for his goodness heretofore'. In 1555 the town again resolved to allow the earl the nomination of one of its members, and to give him a present at the next assizes. Occasionally a borough might find itself in the difficult position of trying to curry favour with two influential men at the same time. In 1553, for instance, Stamford was able to give one nomination to William Cecil, and another to a local gentleman, but found that it had to refuse a third request from the lord admiral. In the same year Grantham wrote to Cecil, who had asked the borough for two nominations:

your desire in your said letter touching the appointing of one of our burgesses we have most gladly accepted and granted, and have requested the sheriff to repair unto you for the nomination of the person, . . . for the other . . . at the special suit of the earl of Rutland we have agreed to continue our ancient {i.e. former] burgess . . . so that we be not able to perform your request.

Moreover, parliamentary meetings imposed a heavy financial burden on many boroughs. Members were entitled to wages of 4s. a day if they were knights of the shire and 2s. a day if burgesses. In addition, members might claim expenses—the cost of their travel, their lodging in London, the enrolment of their election writ, and the cost of securing copies of bills in which they were interested. Thus, one of the members for Exeter in 1558 was paid £10 wages, reimbursed £47 expenses, and also compensated by £2. 13s. 4d. for the loss of his horse. Tips and presents could amount to quite a large sum: the city of Worcester, which had promoted a bill in 1572 'touching a water course', paid 10s. for the drafting of the bill, 3s. 4d. for its engrossment, 5s. for the drawing of a proviso, 4s. for two cheeses 'bestowed about the same matter' on the speaker, and 10s. to the clerk of the parliament for engrossing the bill after its second reading. (The bill was rejected.)

Worcester and Exeter were rich enough to bear such burdens, but many smaller boroughs wilted under the strain: the unprecedented length of the Reformation Parliament, which is estimated to have cost as much as £70 for each burgess, was for some boroughs the last straw. Offers such as that made in 1539 to Guildford by the earl of Southampton, that his client would serve without wages or expenses, were therefore readily accepted. The earl of Rutland's nominees who represented Lincoln in the 1550s served without wages. Dunwich, with an annual income of only £50, was very willing in 1559 to accept Sir Edmund Rowse's offer to serve 'freely without receiving any wages'. (Rowse later went back on his promise, suing the borough in chancery for £19. 4s.) In 1584 Gloucester felt able to resist the earl of Leicester's suggestion that if the city accepted his nominee no wages would be demanded, but the fact that the offer was made is itself revealing:

by that time most boroughs had succumbed to pressure from outside.

Magnates rarely intervened in order to promote a townsman, although they occasionally did so on behalf of the borough's recorder. Rather, they wanted seats for their relatives and their clients, that is, for gentlemen. Boroughs were in general willing to be represented by non-resident gentlemen, despite a statute of 1413 which required that representatives should on the day of issue of the writ of summons be resident in the shire or borough which they sought to represent. There were two main reasons for the boroughs' willingness to accept such interlopers. One was that true townsmen were often reluctant to leave their businesses and shops for the expensive and unhealthy capital, whereas in the sixteenth century gentlemen were increasingly attracted by London. Secondly, it was to a borough's advantage to have a man of influence and *savoir-faire* as its representative at Westminster.

Meetings of parliament were occasions on which a great deal of useful business could be done outside as well as inside the chamber: lawsuits in which a municipality was involved might be given a discreet nudge, civil servants could be approached, magnates might be consulted. In the 1550s, for instance, the members for York were told to discover what was happening to cases pending in the exchequer, to attempt to reduce the city's tax assessment, and to persuade the queen to contribute towards the upkeep of the hospital of St Thomas. For all this they were to seek the assistance of the earl of Shrewsbury. The need to do business, the need to have friends at court, made boroughs anxious to find representatives with sufficient social standing to sway powerful men. This was clearly recognized in a debate that arose in 1571, when it was discovered that Thomas Long had secured his return for Westbury by bribing the mayor and another elector. There was general discussion of the kind of men who should be elected to the Commons, and someone suggested that there were boroughs too small to produce men of the right kind. To this another member replied that there was no real problem: 'I can never be persuaded but that either the lord, whose the town is, . . . or the steward, if that it be the queen's, or some good gentleman of the county adjacent will assign' them someone suitable. Here was a clear recognition both of magnate patronage and of the fact that a borough might be better served with a gentleman as its representative than with a humble townsman. From an early date boroughs had regarded the main duty of their parliamentary representative as being to act as their attorney and undertake town business at Westminster;[4] they therefore welcomed the support of well-connected lawyers and gentlemen.

For these social and financial reasons, then, boroughs were open to influence by magnates. This was nothing new. From the late fourteenth century magnates can frequently be found interfering in elections in order to secure the return of their clients: in the North, for example, the Nevilles and the Percies dominated the constituencies, and 'nomination by their stewards at the county court was almost normal'.[5] In East Anglia, Mowbrays, de la Poles, and de Veres held sway, and John Paston had frequently to defend the right of the Norfolk gentlemen against the nomination of the nobility's 'menial servants'. The duke of York had at least four of his followers in the parliament of 1450, and Lord Hastings seven in 1478.[6] Noble influence continued, and perhaps extended, in the sixteenth century: J. K. Gruenfelder, in his study of influence in early Stuart elections, argues that between 1604 and 1628 the peerage was involved in from 38 to 48 per cent of all elections, and secured 24–30 per cent of all seats for its nominees.[7]

The greatest patron of all was, naturally, the monarch. In some constituencies the monarch was lord of the manor: Steyning after 1539 was such a borough, providing seats for crown servants and lawyers in all the Marian parliaments except one. The crown could also influence a number of boroughs through their officials. The warden of the Cinque Ports, for instance, had considerable power in the constituencies under his directions; in New Romney the warden reversed the borough's choice in 1553, putting in his own man 'contrary to the town's election'. In 1554 the borough of Winchelsea agreed that the lord warden 'shall have the presentation of the burgesses for the parliament for this time'. And so it went on. In 1584 the warden was directed to secure the return of men 'known to be well affected in religion and towards the present state of this government'. In 1593 and 1601 New Romney gave the warden the nomination of one of its burgesses.

A very important source of royal patronage was the duchy of Lancaster boroughs, some of which were in Lancashire, the remainder scattered from Monmouth to East Anglia. The chancellors of the duchy were always loyal crown officials, and duchy seats were usually filled by civil servants and lawyers: in 1555, for instance, the representatives of the duchy borough of Ripon were described, correctly, as having been 'appointed' by the chancellor, who often received blank returns into which he inserted suitable names.

The government, of course, might also intervene in boroughs where the monarch had no special position. The most notorious example of such intervention was the Canterbury election of 1536. The city had already proceeded to an election when a letter arrived from the council directing the borough to re-elect the members who had attended the Reformation Parliament. Cromwell wrote to the sheriff telling him that the council's nominees should be returned if the city intended 'to avoid his highness's displeasure'; the sheriff duly assembled ninety-seven people, and in a fresh election the government nominees were chosen.

In this instance the government had initially tried to influence all elections, borough and shire, through the device of 'circular letters', that is, letters sent out with the writs instructing sheriffs to secure the return of men of a particular sort. In 1536 the letters had asked that 'such personages may be elected as shall serve and for their worship and qualities be most meet for this purpose [i.e. discussion of the succession]'. Letters of this kind were sent before the second Edwardian parliament, and before Mary's third parliament of 1554, when electors were told to choose men of 'the wise, grave and catholic sort, such as indeed mean the true honour of God with the prosperity of the commonswealth'. No letters seem to have been sent before Mary's fourth parliament, but a circular was issued before the last in 1558, asking for the election of men 'of gravity and knowledge in their own counties and towns'. Elizabeth does not appear to have used circular letters for her early parliaments, but the practice was revived in 1571. In 1586, electors were advised to re-elect the members chosen in 1584, and circular letters were also issued before the parliament of 1597 asking, like those of 1558, for the return of local men.

We cannot tell how much influence letters of this sort had. In Mary's reign some returns do explicitly state that, as the queen had requested, men of 'the wise, grave and catholic sort' had been elected, but this often means no more than that the men chosen for the previous parliament had been elected again; there was no change in the pattern of election. The request before the 1586 parliament that men who had sat in 1584 should be chosen again seems to have produced a higher rate of re-election than usual, although 48 per cent of seats were none the less occupied by new men. It is difficult to know whether circular letters did anything more than provide constituencies with a justification for doing what they wanted to do anyway: as Neale said about 1586, the council's letter may simply have acted as 'a stimulus to old members to seek re-election, where otherwise they must have had to yield place to others'. In Leicestershire, certainly, the letter enabled the earl of Huntingdon to prolong a family monopoly and have two brothers re-elected for the county seats. It is difficult to believe that circular letters were an effective way of controlling elections.

Another way in which the monarch could exert some influence was the scrutiny of returns. Writs were returned to chancery, which had sent them out, and the clerk of the crown in chancery then drew up a list of members. In 1581 the House of Commons became uneasy about this process. A number of seats had become vacant since the parliament had first opened in 1572, and the lord chancellor had issued writs to fill the gaps. The House decided, quite unhistorically, that for the duration of the parliament writs should not go out 'without the warrant of the House, first directed for the same to the clerk of the crown'. In 1586 the House went even further, arguing in the Norfolk election case that only members of the Commons could decide on the validity of returns. However, it retreated somewhat in 1589, and agreed that whilst the scrutiny of returns was the responsibility of chancery, it was for the House to direct the crown office to send a new writ if no return had been made. In 1593 the Commons set up a committee for elections and privileges; this included all privy councillors in the House and thirty others, and seems to have been anxious to work with the lord keeper rather than against him. The 1597 committee was less docile, but its membership again included all councillors, the solicitor-general, the attorney of the duchy of Lancaster, and the master of requests. In 1601, it was the keeper who made the concessions rather than the committee. The problem of the scrutiny of returns was not fully settled until the Buckinghamshire election case of 1604.

The right of scrutiny exercised by the monarch does not appear to have been used in the sixteenth century to exclude members whose political or religious views were unsympathetic to the government. Recognizing that the House of Commons was concerned merely with an assertion of its ability to run its own affairs, crown officials therefore did not resist very strongly the establishment of the committee for returns and privileges.

Besides interference in elections and scrutiny of returns there was one other way in which the crown could influence the composition of the Lower House. This was by the creation of new parliamentary seats. The House of Commons increased in size over the sixteenth century from 296 to 462: Henry VIII added 45 new seats, 31 of them through the enfranchisement of Cheshire and Wales, Edward added 34, Mary 25, and Elizabeth 62. This increase was not a response to population shift or economic change: there was no belief at this period that boroughs that were flourishing had any special claim to representation. Many of the boroughs newly represented in the sixteenth century were decaying, and some, like the Isle of Wight constituencies and Andover, were truly 'rotten'. But this did not worry con-temporaries: indeed, in the 1571 debate discussed above, one member declared that it was particularly important that decayed towns should be represented in the Commons, since the men sitting for such areas would have direct experience of their problems. So how are these enfranchisements to be explained?

A number of theories exist. The traditional view was that the Tudors were trying to 'pack' the Commons, that is, to fill the House with royal nominees. The newer theory, most clearly set out by Sir John Neale, is that the creation of new seats was a response to pressure from magnates who wanted more seats to satisfy the demands of their clients. There is certainly evidence for some magnate pressure: Castle Rising in Norfolk was prob-ably enfranchised at the request of the duke of Norfolk, the earl of Rutland secured the right of representation for East Retford in 1571, although he was unsuccessful in his attempt to secure seats for Newark in 1579, whilst Newport, Isle of Wight, even recorded in the borough archives that it was 'at the special instance of Sir George Carey'—governor of the island and a cousin of the queen— that 'burgesses were admitted in the High Court of Parliament'.

Not every newly created seat can be explained in terms of

magnate pressure, however. It is noteworthy how many of the new seats were in areas of crown influence: they were under the sway of the council of the North, like Thirsk, or of the duchy of Cornwall, like Grampound and Camelford. Others were in manors in royal hands, such as Banbury. Above all, they were duchy of Lancaster boroughs—Preston, Thetford, Liverpool, Wigan, Ripon, Higham Ferrers, Stockbridge, Sudbury, and so on. We have already seen how easily controlled these duchy boroughs were, and all were in fact used to provide seats for useful and experienced crown servants. Tudor monarchs were not interested in anything as systematic as 'packing'—otherwise, they would never have created single-member constituencies where they could have had double ones—but they had a great need for 'useful' men in the House. Increasingly, they needed members who could keep the business of the House moving—privy councillors, lawyers, and the rest. It was the purpose of many of the new constituencies to provide seats for such men.

In the course of the Reformation Parliament, no doubt as a result of an initiative by Thomas Cromwell, a new parliamentary process was developed. This was the by-election, an election taking place during a parliament's lifetime to fill a vacancy that had occurred since the parliament first met. By-elections gave the crown considerable opportunity for patronage: the writ was issued at the instruction of the monarch or his ministers, who had ample time in which to write the necessary letters of recommendation or to speak to the persons of power and influence in the neighbourhood. This fact was clearly recognized by those who disliked what had been done in the Reformation Parliament; one of the demands made by Robert Aske, who was involved in the Pilgrimage of Grace, was that 'if a knight or burgess died during parliament, his room should continue void to the end of the same'. Aske's demand was ignored, and Cromwell's exploitation of the by-election was to be emulated by Northumberland and others.

It is important to stress the point that government influence in the sixteenth century was primarily intended to secure seats for men helpful to the crown, and not to keep out those who were potentially hostile. There are one or two exceptions to this—for instance, in 1529 the government was anxious to wrest control of the election writs from Wolsey, presumably because it feared that the Cardinal might fill the House with his own supporters. In 1539 Cromwell's agents tried to prevent Stephen Gardiner from returning candidates in towns under his sway. In 1552 the privy council forcibly expressed its displeasure when Reading was discovered to have filled a vacant seat with John Seymour, the illegitimate half-brother of the discredited Protector. Seymour's election was cancelled—he was in any case a prisoner in the Tower—and the corporation chose again, this time tactfully going for a privy councillor, Sir John Mason. None the less, the main thrust of the influence exerted by the crown was intended either to produce local men of sound judgement or to find seats for men of specialized skills: lawyers or civil servants. It was intended to improve parliament's efficiency by ensuring that a number of those who sat in the Lower House were experienced men of affairs, rather than to pack the House in the interest of some specific piece of crown policy.

What sort of men were thus elected to the Lower House? The knights of the shire were, of course, the men of weight and influence in their area, and the leaders of country society. What of the burgesses? By statute the burgesses were, as we have seen, required to be residents of the boroughs they represented; in fact, they were frequently not true townsmen at all, but gentlemen, and often gentlemen whose links with the borough they represented were very tenuous. Increasingly, by a process known to historians as 'the gentry invasion of the boroughs', boroughs had come to be represented by men of the same social status as those who had the more prestigious task of sitting for the counties.

This process was by the sixteenth century well-established. In 1478 one-half of known borough members were of gentry status, and townsmen were to make up only about half of the borough members in the Reformation Parliament. In Elizabeth's reign about one-third of borough members were country gentlemen, and another quarter to one-third government officials or lawyers. Only a small proportion were true townsmen: 23 per cent of the burgesses of 1559, 19 per cent in 1571, and 14 per cent in 1601. Thus, whilst some towns such as Cambridge and Bristol persisted throughout the century in returning true townsmen, and most boroughs did so occasionally, the general trend was towards representation by outsiders and by gentlemen.

We have already considered the concerns that prompted boroughs to accept such men as their representatives. Why did gentlemen seek election in ever-increasing numbers? The answer lies partly in social attractions, partly in the pursuit of political advancement.

Parliamentary experience, Sir Geoffrey Elton has argued, could be a means by which the ambitious young man might bring himself to the attention of the monarch.[8] He points to the example of Thomas Cromwell, who said of his own election that he 'had once put in his foot where he trusted shortly to be better regarded', and concludes: 'men who wished to reach the council, men who hoped to help govern the country, needed other means as well and other connections, but increasingly they discovered that they could lay sound foundations by seeking election to parliament'.

However, whilst it is true that, for example, most privy councillors in the sixteenth century had sat in the House of Commons at some earlier stage in their career, that obviously does not in itself prove that it was by means of service in the Commons that they had come to the attention of the crown. Moreover, it is far from clear that members of parliament were, as a group, upwardly mobile. The History of Parliament Trust has shown that in the reign of Elizabeth about as many members were in the process of moving down the social scale as were moving up, and even those who were moving up seem to have done so more frequently through an advantageous marriage than through a lucrative government post.[9] Thus, service in the Commons cannot have been helpful to the careers of more than a handful.

There is, nevertheless, one group for which Elton's theory may be accurate, and that is the lawyers. Parliament does seem to have provided lawyers with an opportunity to display their learning and expertise: twenty of the lawyers in the Commons in 1597, for instance, were subsequently promoted to legal office.[10] Lawyers were certainly very willing to accept an obligation that fitted in well with their legal commitments: in the Reformation Parliament, for example, they formed the largest occupational group after the country gentlemen, and the proportion of lawyers in the House continued to increase under Elizabeth, from 16 per cent to 27 per cent. In 1585 William Fleetwood rather pompously complained that too many of his fellow lawyers were spending the day in the courts, 'neglecting the service of this House'. The Commons eventually resolved to send the serjeant-at-arms to recover its missing members, only to find that Fleetwood himself had disappeared to the court of common pleas. However, the habit of many boroughs of automatically electing their recorders makes it difficult to analyse the extent to which lawyers actively sought seats in the Commons.

Many gentlemen, however, seem to have regarded election in a more light-hearted way. 'I am one that loves to see fashions, and desires to know wonders', was the justification given by one gentleman for his wish to find a seat. The growth of London as a centre of conspicuous consumption, and the development of the London season, undoubtedly added in the later sixteenth century to the attractions of the Commons. Doting fathers, indeed, seem to have regarded parliament as the equivalent of a finishing school, as a means of giving their sons a little 'breeding'. Thus, in 1597 one father wrote: 'as my son is as it were entering into the world and to those years that may fit his country's service . . . I am minded to advise him to stand to be knight of the shire for Surrey against the next parliament'.

It was because the Commons was seen as a mixture of civil service selection board and finishing-school that county families tried to share out its advantages. As the second earl of Pembroke declared in 1572: 'I would have all gentlemen to have their due reserved unto them, which is, from time to time, as parliaments fall out, to be chosen; now some, and then some, as they are fit; to the end they may be [experienced] in the affairs and state of their country'.

One privilege enjoyed by members of parliament was freedom from arrest during the parliamentary sessions, and for a time before and after it. In a litigious age, this was a privilege of some significance. To take but one example, Gabriel Pleydell, a quarrelsome Wiltshire gentleman, sat in only three parliaments, but in two of these (1555 and 1563) he claimed immunity against impending legal actions. Some members clearly abused their privilege, and may indeed have sought election for this purpose. In 1571 the queen's circular letter specifically warned that 'many in late parliaments, Her Majesty thinketh, have been named [i.e. elected] for private respects and favour upon their own suits [or] to enjoy some immunity from arrests upon actions during the time of parliaments'. This warning seems to have gone unheeded. George Gascoigne, the poet, was said in 1572 to have 'lurked at villages' until he was elected as member for Midhurst, whereupon he openly showed his face 'in the despite of all his creditors'. The government agent and spy, William Herle, probably also sought election in 1586 to avoid imprisonment for debt. In 1593 the lord keeper again advised members to be sure that 'the protection of your House be not worn by any man for a cloak to defraud others of their debts and duties'; the incentive for this speech may have been the attempted arrest for debts of over £5,500 of Thomas Fitzherbert, member for Newcastle under Lyme, which led to a lengthy discussion of parliamentary privilege.

Although gentlemen were increasingly interested in a seat in the House of Commons, they were not, when elected, very assiduous in their attendance there. Theoretically, no member should have absented himself without securing a licence. Licences were given for such reasons as family illness or death, or because a lawyer had to attend the assizes or a government official carry out some task in the provinces. However, every time a call, that is, a count, of the House was taken the number of absentees without licence was found to be large, and the story of Carew Raleigh, knight of the shire for Wiltshire in 1585, who, it was said, 'came not at the parliament house all the latter session, but was in the country', may have had a number of parallels. Again and again in the sixteenth century bills were introduced to stop members from absenting themselves without licences, again and again fines were imposed, again and again the House passed weighty statements of disapproval. In November 1554 and in 1581 fines were even imposed on absentees, and in 1571 it was decided that members not present for prayers in the morning should pay 4d. into the poor box. To no avail.

Exactly how many people were present in the House is known only when a counted vote, or division, was taken, for the number discovered at the 'calls' was not recorded. In the early years of Elizabeth's reign, only 276 of the four hundred plus members who had been returned were ever present in a division. In the parliament of 1601 less that half the House was ever present at a division, and in one vote the numbers dropped to eighty. Division figures are likely to give an inflated impression of attendance, since it is probable that more members came when some controversial matter was being hotly debated than would turn up routinely, and these numbers may reflect an uncharacteristically large attendance. The norm was probably much lower.

In trying to explain why men who were enthusiastic about election were reluctant about attendance we have to return to the question of what men sought to gain by their election. What is clear is that their preoccupations were not those of subsequent historians. Sir John Neale, in particular, fell into the trap of thinking of parliaments as primarily political. To go from his account back to the Journals and the diaries of members is to move from the realm of high politics and elevated discussion of abstract political concepts to a much more mundane region, a region of property disputes, street-paving, and the prohibition of foreign hats. Sir Geoffrey Elton has pointed out, for example, that whilst Neale's picture of the parliament of 1576 is dominated by Peter Wentworth and his great defence of freedom of speech, the Journal reveals that far more time was spent both on the floor of the House and in committee on a bill dealing with the lands bequeathed by a private Oxfordshire gentleman, Sir Richard Wenham.[11]

Thus, it is far from clear that contemporaries shared the preoccupation of later historians with questions relating to religion, the succession, and the constitution. Their priorities were different. In the last session of the Reformation Parliament, for example, the passage of an extremely important bill concerning the government of Calais was held up by Sir Richard Whetall's efforts to ensure that it contained a clause giving his son a reversion to a minor office there. Contemporaries do not seem to have regarded this as improper. The next parliament spent a great deal of time on the details of a lease of a marsh outside Calais. Indeed, much parliamentary time, not only in the sixteenth century but also in the seventeenth and eighteenth centuries, was taken up with what may loosely be called private legislation, that is, legislation dealing with disputed inheritances, with marriage settlements and the like. For some members, these bills may have been the main reason for their presence in parliament. In 1542, for example, Sir Gilbert Talbot, sitting as knight of the shire for Worcestershire, secured an act confirming his right to the manor of Grafton, whilst Sir Ralph Sadler, who represented Preston in 1545, obtained in that parliament an act legitimatizing his children. At a different social level, the 1554 act for the making of russels (a kind of cloth) mentions as its originators the two members for Norwich, John Corbet and Alexander Mather, both clothiers with a direct interest in the proposals they sponsored.

Boroughs too, were often more interested in their own concerns than with matters of national importance. In the reign of Edward, a reign in which numerous statutes were passed fundamentally altering the church, the corporation at York was far more concerned about securing legislation to prevent the destruction of wood within sixteen miles of the city, to stop butchers grazing within six miles of the city, and to forbid the manufacture of coloured cloth north of the Trent outside the city, than with the statutes in which historians have been most interested. The representatives themselves, writing back about the parliament, reported the passing of a bill for the uniting of two parishes in York but did not mention either the first or the second Edwardian Prayer Book.

Gentlemen did not seek election at this period, then, because they had some burning desire to reform either church or state, but because they felt that a seat in the House of Commons was a proper reflection of their status. Exchanges between clients and patrons, between constituencies and candidates, were therefore framed in terms of 'service', not of policy. An anonymous Elizabethan letter to a patron, for instance, said: 'I am bold to become a humbler suitor unto you to help to place me a burgess on your country [county], where it shall seem to you best. Your honour shall command me and my service.' In 1593 Sir George Savile told one of his friends to turn up and vote for him as knight of the shire for Yorkshire, with 'such freeholders out of Craven as you can persuade to be there and give me their voices'; in return, he said that he would be 'ever ready to requite . . . your favours'. Obedience, fealty, duty, service: these are the words most frequently used in such correspondence. Clients wanted seats in the House of Commons for their 'learning's sake', magnates wanted their clients to have seats in order to display their own importance, and boroughs were vulnerable to both.

3

Procedure

Parliament usually met in London, and began with a splendid procession to Westminster Abbey led by the monarch, with the peers in their scarlet and ermine parliament robes and the bishops in scarlet with lawn sleeves. The procession would then return to the White Chamber of the Palace of Westminster, where the chancellor (or lord keeper) would set out, briefly, the main reasons for which the parliament had been summoned. The two Houses would then separate, the Lords to register absentees and their proxies, the Commons to elect their speaker.

Thereafter, the two Houses assembled separately: the Lords in the White Chamber, the Commons, at first, in the chapter house or the refectory of Westminster Abbey. In the reign of Edward VI, however, the Commons acquired St Stephen's chapel for their meetings. The layout of that building, and, in particular, of its antechamber, was to have an important effect on the way in which procedure developed in the Lower House.

The Lords' Chamber was oblong, with the throne at one end. When the monarch was not present, the chancellor sat in front of the throne, on a wool sack. Before him sat the clerk of the parliament and the clerk of the crown, with a table to work on, and, kneeling, one or two assistants. Beyond, on wool sacks covered with red cloth, sat the judges and other legal officials. To the right of the throne was a bench for the archbishops and bishops. On the left were two similar benches, with the dukes, marquises, earls, and viscounts on the inner one, and the barons next to the wall; they also filled the cross-bench on the fourth wall. The seating plan, at least on formal occasions, observed strict conventions: the bishops of London, Durham, and Winchester sat nearest to the throne, with the other bishops placed according to the date of their appointment. The peers were seated according to the date of the creation of their title, except that from 1539 the king's officers of state had precedence over all other peers save royal dukes: several of the parliaments of this period witnessed bitter dissension between peers over questions of precedence, such as that between Lord Clifford and Lord Fitzwalter in 1523. At the end of the room was the 'bar', or rail, which marked off a space into which could come members of the Lower House, or other suitors.

From the end of the fourteenth century the Commons used the refectory of the monks of Westminster for their meetings.[1] This was a long, thin room, with a fixed high table at one end. Whether the other tables customarily used by the monastic community stayed in place around the walls during meetings is not clear, but it seems probable that most members had to stand: the seats that were installed when the Commons acquired the chapel of St Stephen's may have themselves contributed to the increasing length of debates. The chapel, when fully converted for the Commons' use, was oblong, 'made like a Theatre, having four rows of seats one above another round about the same'. At one end was the speaker's chair, with a table before it for the under-clerk of the parliament, otherwise known as the clerk of the Commons. The privy councillors and other government officials sat close to the speaker's chair, but otherwise no one could claim a seat of prescriptive right. Next to the Chamber was an antechamber, in which the clerks usually sat, and suitors and others waited, but when a division took place the room had to be emptied for voters.

By the end of the century the number of suitors and attendants hanging around outside the Chamber was causing serious problems. 'The lewd misdemeanours of pages and other unruly persons' on the stairs and in the passage was disgraceful, Sir Francis Hastings told the House in 1601, for 'not only abuse is offered, but weapons and blood drawn'. A conference was called between the two Houses, and agreement was reached about which attendants could remain outside the Chamber.

Traditionally, both Houses sat in the mornings only, and not on Sunday. The Lords at the beginning of the period sat from 9 a.m. to twelve or one, and the Commons, about whom we know less until their Journal began in 1547, probably met from eight to eleven. However, as the century went on, the press of business made afternoon sessions more and more necessary. None the less, in the reign of Elizabeth, it was customary for the Upper Chamber to avoid, if it could, meetings on Wednesday and Friday mornings during the law term, when the court of Star Chamber sat, and when convocation met.

The Commons' first task was to elect a speaker. The privy council in fact made the choice: in 1553, for instance, the duke of Northumberland wrote to the lord chamberlain reminding him to get on with the task of selection so that the man appointed might have an opportunity to prepare his speech of acceptance. (In 1584 Burghley even wrote his opening speech for him.) It was normally one of the councillors in the Commons who would nominate the person decided upon: in 1563, for instance, the treasurer declared that, in his opinion, Mr Thomas Williams was the best man for the job, and the rest of the House agreed, shouting out 'Mr Williams, Mr Williams'. Although the man chosen knew that his name was going to be proposed, and had, indeed, already written his speech, it was customary for him to appear reluctant. He would explain that he was unworthy of the honour, and would implore the House to choose again. Finally, he would be persuaded into acceptance. Later, when presented to the monarch, he would repeat some of his modest disclaimers. Thus Yelverton in 1597 said:

Your speaker ought to be a man big and comely, stately and well-spoken, his voice great, his carriage majestic, his nature haughty and his purse plentiful . . . But . . . the stature of my body is small, myself not so well-spoken, my voice low, my carriage of the common fashion, my nature soft and bashful, my purse thin, light and never plentiful.

From the 1550s we know that the speaker routinely finished his oration by asking for 'free speech in the house, privilege from arrest and troubles for the common House and their servants', and the right of access to the monarch; it is probable similar requests were made earlier in the century.

The speaker was paid £100 a session by the monarch, and £5 for each private bill passed and enacted. (Some boroughs also paid him for 'pains' taken on their behalf.) No one at this time seems to have been concerned about the fact that the speaker was a royal nominee. In 1566, it is true, the choice of Onslow was debated, and a vote taken, but this was because, as solicitor-general, he already had a place in the Lords.

Most of the speakers of this period were lawyers, and after 1523 they all were. Indeed, not until the election of Sir Edward

Seymour in 1673 was a non-lawyer to become speaker again. The first speaker not to be a knight of the shire was Humphrey Wingfield, who succeeded Sir Thomas Audley in the course of the Reformation Parliament.

The role of the speaker, as described by John Hooker in 1571, was 'to direct and guide that House in good order, and to see the ordinances, usages, and customs' of the House were observed, to see 'the record truly to be entered and to be safely kept by the clerk'. He received the bills brought into the House, chose the order in which they were read, and decided when a vote should be taken. He thus fixed the timetable of the House, and controlled its proceedings. The Commons could not meet without him, and since there was at this time no deputy speaker, his sickness or absence at a meeting with the monarch meant that business had to be suspended (see below, pp. 142–3).

The speaker could, theoretically, join in the debate only if the House consented. Consent was usually forthcoming: in 1593, for example, the speaker added to a discussion of a case of privilege some words about 'a parliament held by Edward son of Edward'. However, earlier, in 1581, the Puritan Anthony Cope had complained that the speaker had 'on some such matters as he hath favoured, but without licence of this House, . . . spoken to a bill, and in some other cases which he did not favour or like of, he would prejudice the speeches of other members'.

Similar tasks were carried out in the Lords by the chancellor or lord keeper. He arranged the course of each day's business, and tried to maintain decorum in the Chamber. The chancellor received no gratuity for his service in the Lords, but he was paid for each private bill enacted, at a rate which was by the early seventeenth century £10 a bill.

Bills were introduced by individual members of either House, who gave them to the lord keeper, or to the speaker. Bills might stem from private initiative, from some borough, institution, or occupation, or from the government. Frequently, an informal committee of the privy council was set up before a session to consider the legislative programme that would be laid before the parliament. Some constituencies seem to have made similar preparations: in York, for example, the mayor normally summoned the aldermen and part of the common council and asked if there was any business they wanted their burgesses to prefer. Sometimes, too, bills were drafted in the course of the session by committees in response to a need that had become clear in the course of the meeting.

There is no very clear pattern about where bills were first read, although the bill for lay taxation was always introduced into the Commons, and the bill for clerical taxation into the Lords; bills of attainder and related matters, bills of pardon, and proposals relating to individual peers usually began in the Lords. Michael Graves suggested in 1981, however, that a change came about in the Lords' initiating role in the 'first two years and three parliaments of Mary's reign', a period in which he perceived 'a disturbed political climate'.[2] Even if Graves is in the short term correct— and not all historians would agree with him—it is clear from studies of the reign of Elizabeth that the Lords retained a considerable legislative initiative, although, of course, the much larger size of the Lower House meant that the majority of bills started there. What seems to have mattered most, as Sir Geoffrey Elton has pointed out, was 'the place in which the council's leading parliamentary manager sat':[3] for example, important bills began in the Commons when Thomas Cromwell sat there, but in the Lords when he was elevated in 1539, and they similarly moved when William Cecil became Lord Burghley.[4]

Bills were normally read, or discussed, three times on three separate occasions, and then were sent to the other House for the procedure to be repeated. Controversial measures might receive more than three readings, but the general trend over the century was towards uniformity in this matter. The clerk of the Commons was responsible for the first—and literal—reading of a bill in the Lower House and the clerk of the parliament in the Lords; the measure's purport was then explained by the speaker or chancellor. (Those members who had a particular interest in the proposal could procure a copy of the bill: for this the clerk charged, in 1571, a penny per ten lines.) First readings were largely a formality, and it was at the time of the second reading that debate would take place.

Despite the existence of conventions governing debate, some discussions in the Chamber were very disorderly. It was the task of the speaker to control debate, to determine who should speak, and if anyone spoke irrelevantly, to 'will him to come to the matter'. These were not easy tasks, for members were often intolerant of others' weaknesses: boring speeches, or those by unpopular members, might be greeted by spitting and shuffling of feet. In 1572, for example, Arthur Hall was treated to such 'shuffling of feet and hawking' that he could not be heard, and at Mr Heyle's speech on the subsidy in 1601 the House 'hemmed and laughed and talked'. The speaker sternly observed that 'it is the ancient use of every one to be silent when anyone speaketh', but when Heyle went on to cite precedents from 'the times of Henry III, John, Stephen etc', more 'hemming' broke out. Later in that same parliament an old doctor of civil law spoke, and 'because he was too long, and spake too low, the House hawked and spat'. Sir Francis Hastings delivered the reproof this time, observing that the House should listen to each of its members with attention, 'though he speak never so absurdly'.

If the debate suggested that there was support for the proposal it was either 'engrossed', that is, written on parchment instead of paper, or 'committed', that is, a committee of the House was set up in order to look at the proposal in more detail. In the early sixteenth century, committees to revise bills were infrequent: only six of the forty-eight bills discussed by the Lords in 1510 were committed, for example. In the period 1536–47 less than one-fifth of the bills read in the Lords were committed. Even in the early part of Elizabeth's reign the process remained relatively rare, but by the end of the sixteenth century it was, perhaps, the norm. Committees enabled groups of members to consider several matters at the same time, a more and more necessary task as the business of parliament grew. Moreover, the general rules governing debate were suspended, and a freer discussion was thus facilitated.

After debate, engrossment, and, sometimes, committal, bills received their third reading, and were put to the vote. Peers voted individually, 'content' or 'not content'. If, despite his 'not content', a bill was passed, a peer could register a formal protest against a proposal, a privilege that peers frequently used and seem to have taken seriously. In the Commons, the vote was by acclamation: members shouted 'yea' or 'no', and the speaker decided which response was the louder. Only if he could not decide, or his decision was challenged, would there be a counted vote. (Voting in the Commons thus closely resembled that at elections.) Counted votes seem to have taken place in the Chamber itself in the early sixteenth century, and may have resembled the 'view' taken by a sheriff at a contested election, but after the Commons acquired St Stephen's chapel a procedure developed which came to be known as the 'division'.[5] Divisions involved the affirmative party leaving the Chamber, and going into an antechamber; they were counted as they re-entered. The noes were counted in their seats, a system that militated against the affirmative party. The Chamber could not provide seats for all, and members were reluctant to risk losing their places: in 1601 Mr Martin declared:

I have observed it, that ever this parliament, the noes upon division of the House have carried it. The reason whereof, as I conceive it is, because divers are loth to go forth for losing of their places, and many that cry I, will sit still with the Noes.

The speaker did not vote. In 1601, after discussion of a bill for compulsory attendance at church, the House came to a division. The yeas 'went forth, and were 105, and the Noes within, 106'. The question then arose of whether the speaker could vote. Sir Edward Hoby declared that since he was an elected member he could, but Sir Walter Ralegh and the speaker himself dissented, arguing that 'he was to be indifferent for both parties'. The chancellor, on the other hand, provided that he was a peer in his own right, could vote, leaving the Woolsack to do so. The judges and other legal assistants did not vote, however.

A bill's passage in the second Chamber would usually be less time-consuming than in the first, although bills were often amended in the second House, and, at least at the end of the century, often committed a second time. Sometimes the second Chamber rejected a bill passed by the first, and sometimes it replaced the proposal by one of its own, which would then have to be reread and passed by the other House.

Thomas Smith noted in the 1560s that if difficulties arose between the two Houses over a bill, representatives from both Houses would meet 'so each part be informed of [the] other's meaning. After which meeting for the most part . . . either part agree to others bills'. In the early Tudor period such joint meetings were usually concerned with weighty 'commonwealth' matters, such as, in 1554, the drafting of a petition asking for reunion with Rome, or the subsidy, although occasionally meetings took place to deal with more routine bills, such as the joint conference of 1544 to deal with the king's style, which was ordered to meet at 8 a.m. 'in cubiculo parliamenti'. However, in 1571, at the Lords' initiative, it was agreed that conferences should be held to sort out the difficulties of a number of bills, and in the last four weeks of that parliament sixteen such meetings were held. Thereafter, conferences were very common: over seven bills in 1584–5, eleven in 1589, and so on. Indeed, some resentment was felt by the Lords when the Commons replaced their bills without first seeking a conference. Although from time to time conferences were unable to sort out all the problems caused by a particular measure, they usually resulted in agreement.

Whilst these meetings were useful, they also had their dangers. Meetings were always held on the Lords' territory, in the Painted Chamber, the council room, or the outer chamber of the Lords' House. Members from the Lower House had to stand, bareheaded, whereas the peers sat with their hats on. As conferences dealt with more and more detailed matter, and became longer and longer, this distinction perhaps came to be more resented: in James's first parliament there were complaints about 'the long and painful standing', and a suggestion that members 'found themselves sick and lame long after'. There were obvious dangers for the Commons in a situation which so firmly emphasized the social hierarchy, and in 1572 one commentator declared that 'no one thing has so shaken the true liberty of the House as often conferences'. He believed that members of the Lower House meeting peers and learning their 'inclinations', and 'knowing that in the Commons House there is nothing secret', were prone to change their attitudes. However, the utility of conferences clearly outweighed such doubts.

Of course, even with frequent meetings, relations between the two Houses could still occasionally be strained. The Commons sometimes stood upon their dignity: in 1597, for instance, the two Houses had an acrimonious dispute about the precise form in which the Lords added amendments to bills that had already passed the Commons, which led the peers to observe that it did not matter much 'whether such amendments be written in parchment or in paper, either white paper, black paper or brown paper'. The Lords sometimes grew impatient with what they regarded as the Commons' slow conduct of business: from 1515, when the Commons were instructed to bring along all the bills that had passed their House but not yet come before the Upper House in order that agreement could be reached about which 'should be admitted or dropped', the peers constantly pressed the Commons to process bills quickly. However, in general, and despite the Commons' growing self-confidence and vociferous-ness, relations between the two Houses were good in the sixteenth century. Many of those in the Lords were, of course, relatives or patrons of those in the Commons—'our followers, servants and kinsmen', as Salisbury declared in 1610—and some of the Commons would go on themselves to sit in the Upper House, where they were doubtless often able to enlighten their colleagues about procedure in the Lower House and other such matters. Where links between the two Houses were so close, conflict was unlikely.

Despite the increasing tendency of procedure in the Lower Chamber to mirror that of the Upper, there remained one or two areas in which the two Houses had different functions, and therefore different ways of proceeding. In the case of money bills, for instance, the role of the Commons was much more important than that of the Lords. The Commons, as representatives, bound others to the payment of the taxes they granted, whereas the peers bound only themselves. Until the 1390s taxes had been granted by both Lords and Commons, but in 1407 Henry IV acknowledged that it was the House of Commons which made the grant of taxation, the Lords merely assenting to it. Even the act granting tonnage and poundage differentiated between the representative Commons, who 'grant by this present indenture', and the peers, who 'assent'. Money bills, drafted by the council or by a committee of the House dominated by councillors, were always in the sixteenth century introduced in the Lower House, and were rarely altered by the Lords. The Commons were sensitive about their privileges in this area, and liked to have a little ceremony at the end of the session which involved their speaker giving the bill to the monarch personally or to his representative.

If both Houses agreed to the measure, it would then await the monarch's assent at the end of the session. Not all bills did receive

the royal assent, of course. We are told that at the end of the
famous speech of 1545 in which he complained about 'the word
of God' being 'disputed, rhymed, sung and jangled in every ale-
house and tavern', Henry VIII gave his consent to many bills, but
'divers he assented not unto'. It is impossible to be definitive
about the veto in the period before the Commons Journal, but it
seems as if Henry in fact used it only rarely—in 1540, for
example, the only bill known to have been vetoed was one
attacking the merchant adventurers. Elizabeth, on the other
hand, exercised her right of veto very frequently, with twelve
bills being refused in the parliament of 1597. Indeed, in the
second part of her reign, more official bills failed in this way than
at any other stage in the legislative process.

The bills thus failing cover an extraordinary range of topics,
from the better-observing of the sabbath to the width of mesh of
nets used for the taking of herrings, sprats, and smelts in Orford
Haven. Sir Geoffrey Elton has suggested that Elizabeth mainly
used her veto against bills which she believed would lead to
widespread dissatisfaction, as a 'last defence against ill-
considered, partisan, or even corruptly obtained acts of parliament', and this is probably true of her predecessors as well.[6]

During the parliamentary session, and for a limited period before
and after it, members of both Houses assumed certain rights and
privileges. They were protected against litigation in lower
courts, and they and their servants could not be arrested for
matters such as debt. They enjoyed liberty of speech within the
Chamber, for 'there is no greater enemy to good council than
fear, when men speak either in fear, or fear to speak', as one
member put it in 1593. To preserve this liberty, members had
themselves to maintain silence about their proceedings, which
they were not always able to do. In 1601 Robert Cecil declared
himself to be very shocked by hearing 'parliament matters'
discussed in the streets. The greatest threat to this liberty in the
sixteenth century was not, however, the 'popularity' about
which Cecil complained, but rather the carrying to the monarch
of tales about what members had done and said.

In 1576, for instance, Peter Wentworth's great attack on
'rumours and messages' arose out of Elizabeth's attempts to
control what was discussed in the Lower House, and how it was

discussed. Edward Hoby, very critical in 1589 of abuses in the exchequer, requested specifically that 'speeches used in this House by members of the same be not by any of them made or used as table-talk, or in any wise delivered in notes of writing to any person or persons whatsoever not being members of this House'. It subsequently emerged that Hoby had been reprimanded 'very sharply . . . for some his speeches' by Burghley, who, as a peer and not a member of the Commons, should not have been in a position to know what had gone on in the Lower Chamber. The monopolies debates of 1597 and 1601 produced a number of similar complaints. In fact, whilst always ready to pay lip-service to the principle of freedom of speech, provided that it was neither licentious nor treasonable, Elizabeth consistently attempted to discover what was being said and by whom, and to shape debate according to her desires.

At the same time as parliament met, the convocation of the English church in the province of Canterbury assembled. (The convocation of the province of York usually met after parliament had ended.) Convocation consisted of two houses. In the upper house sat the archbishop of Canterbury and the bishops, abbots, and priors. In the lower house were the archdeacons, two clerical proctors from each of the eighteen dioceses in the province, and various representatives of the cathedral clergy. The formal decisions of convocation, its canons, required the assent of both houses, but, unlike parliamentary statutes, they did not require royal ratification. Although the clergy had often claimed that canons of convocation were of equal weight to acts of parliament, the laity had never accepted that claim. Moreover, the fact that the bishops and monastic heads also had seats in the Upper House of parliament meant that in practice the real battles of this period were fought there.

Convocation met at either Blackfriars or St Paul's, or in Westminster Abbey, probably in the chapter house. Usually its meetings were confined to Monday and Friday, so that members of the upper house could attend the Lords: Hooker tells us that for the same reason the upper house of convocation sat in the afternoons only. Events in convocation thus often served as a complicated counterpoint to what was going on in parliament.

4

Parliaments, 1485–1536

The parliaments of Henry VII's reign, and, indeed, those of Henry VIII before 1529, were very like those of the Yorkists. They were less politically important than parliaments had been earlier in the fifteenth century, and both their place in the constitution and their procedure were a great deal less clear-cut than they were later to become. Parliaments were still only one amongst the various consultative bodies upon which a monarch could call: five great councils were summoned in Henry VII's reign, for instance, and three of these authorized a financial grant, although, as we have already noted, such grants had subsequently to be validated by a parliament.

The king's control of parliament was at this period almost total. In the parliament of 1478, for example, no one had opposed Edward IV when he accused his own brother, the duke of Clarence, of treason, and the speaker had even asked on behalf of the Commons that execution should be hastened. Henry VII never found it necessary to veto a bill, because no measure of which he disapproved could reach the stage of presentation. No royal ministers were impeached after 1450; even then, the supposedly weak Henry VI had been able to stop the impeachment of his chief minister, William de la Pole, substituting for it a sentence of banishment. Parliament in fact made no attempt to control the monarch's choice of servants between 1450 and 1621, the criticisms of Empson and Dudley in the parliament of 1510 being initiated by Henry VIII himself.

The monarch was therefore able to use his parliaments to strengthen his position. Richard III, for example, used the authority of parliament publicly to rehearse his claim to the throne, and to give it formal approval. Similarly, Henry VII used his first parliament to secure a statute which 'ordained, established and enacted' that the inheritance of the crown lay in him and his heirs. The prime object of this statute was to ensure that the monarch's title could not be challenged in the courts, and that his tenure of royal property would be unquestioned; Henry's granddaughters would later pass similar bills to confirm their titles after the complication of Henry VIII's matrimonial entanglements.

The monarchs of this period also secured the passage of a large number of acts of attainder, that is, of statutes declaring an individual or group of people guilty of treason. Acts of attainder form the largest group of public statutes passed in Henry VII's reign, exceeding the number of acts dealing with trade, prices and wages, or law enforcement. Henry VII attainted only 138 people, compared with Edward IV's 140 in a shorter reign, and the attainders of forty-six of these were later reversed, but Henry was unlike Edward in that the process continued and indeed accelerated in the later years of his reign. Each new conspiracy against the king was followed by punitive action in parliament, and the only parliament of the reign without attainders was that of 1497. Opposition to wholesale attainders was, however, voiced in parliament in 1485, when some of those in the Commons were reluctant to condemn Richard III and his supporters at Bosworth Field: 'there was many gentlemen against it', a contemporary recorded, but the bill was none the less passed, 'for it was the king's pleasure'.

A large number of acts passed in these years dealt with restitutions in blood and resumptions of lands confiscated, a consequence of the earlier civil wars. Of 192 statutes passed in Henry VII's reign, forty were acts of resumption, attainder, or restitution. Indeed, Henry's parliaments were marked by a high level of private-act legislation—an average of nineteen per session, compared with only eight under his son, and thirteen under Elizabeth. Although some important pieces of social and economic legislation were implemented in these years, including the first statutory attempts to deal with engrossment and enclosure, Henry VII's parliaments were much more concerned with the needs of the monarch and his greater subjects than they were with the good of the country as a whole.

It is difficult to pass any judgement on the early parliaments of Henry VIII's reign: they were not well recorded, and are now remembered largely for events that foreshadow those of the 1530s. In 1512, for instance, a statute was passed limiting benefit of clergy in cases of robbery and murder to men in 'holy orders', that is, priests, deacons, and subdeacons. This measure remained in force only until the next parliament, that of 1515, by which time resentment of clerical privilege had been exacerbated by the 'Hunne affair'. Richard Hunne was a London merchant who had refused in 1511 to pay a mortuary fee to his rector on the death of his baby son. The rector sued for his fee in the archbishop's court, which found for him. Hunne responded by attacking the rector in the court of King's Bench under the 1393 statute of praemunire, which forbade any exercise of spiritual jurisdiction which had not been sanctioned by English law. Bishop Fitzjames of London then charged Hunne with heresy, and he was committed to the bishop's prison where he was subsequently found hanged. The church authorities claimed that Hunne had committed suicide: they proceeded with the heresy case, found him guilty, and burnt his corpse.

However, many contemporaries, especially in London, believed that Hunne had not taken his own life, but had been murdered by ecclesiastical officials, and there was considerable support amongst the Commons in the parliament of 1515 for the renewal of the 1512 act restricting benefit of clergy. When the proposal came before the Lords, however, the bishop of London was able to use the spiritual majority in the Upper Chamber to block it. Tempers were not helped by a sermon preached at Paul's Cross on the text 'touch not mine anointed' by the abbot of Winchcombe, nor by a formal debate arranged by Henry himself, in which the warden of the London Franciscans, Standish, defended the general principle of bringing criminous clerks into the secular courts; during the parliamentary recess Standish was himself charged with heresy. The Lower House was furious, but, as Sir Geoffrey Elton has pointed out, its fury achieved little: the 1512 act was not renewed, and moves in parliament to assist Hunne's children came to nothing.[1] Standish himself escaped the heresy charge, but his career was blighted.

The clerk of the parliaments closed his account of the 1515 session with regret for the conflict 'inter clericum et secularem potestatem, super libertatibus ecclesiasticis', yet religious affairs did not at all trouble Henry's next parliament, that of 1523. Only in retrospect does the hostility towards the clergy shown by the Commons in 1512 and 1515 appear ominous.

Both the first two Tudors were interested in parliament as a source of money, although Henry VIII, with an expensive and aggressive foreign policy, was more dependent upon taxation than his frugal father. In 1487 parliament made Henry VII a grant to defray the cost of suppressing Lambert Simnel's revolt, and two years later another to assist Brittany in her fight against France. In 1491 Henry was granted more money for the war against France. The grant of 1497 was so large that it produced a rising in Cornwall. In 1504, however, when Henry asked for two feudal aids, one for the knighting of his elder son, Arthur (who was by that time not only already knighted but also dead), and the other for the marriage of his eldest daughter, he did encounter some difficulty. The Commons, whilst admitting the legality of the request, opposed it, declaring that trying to raise so large a sum would cause 'great vexatious trouble and unquietness'. Hostility to the grant probably arose from the fear that its levy would involve a searching enquiry into the feudal obligations of all landowners which the Commons thought might later be used for other purposes. In the end a grant was agreed of £40,000, to be assessed and collected in the same way as parliamentary taxes; Henry, anxious to conciliate, then decided to take only £30,000.

When the lord chancellor asked parliament in 1512 for money to pay for Henry VIII's invasion of France the request was not well received, some of the Lower House disliking even the idea of the invasion, let alone the cost. In the end, however, Henry was granted two fifteenths and tenths, augmented later in the parliament by the new tax called the subsidy (see above, p. 16). In both sessions of the 1515 parliament taxation was granted without any serious difficulty, perhaps because the simultaneous introduction of a measure revoking some of the grants of office, annuities, and customs licences made since 1509 suggested that the king was willing to place 'the welfare of the generality of his subjects above the favour of particular persons'.[2]

In June 1522 Henry once again went to war with France, raising the money initially by a forced loan. Parliament was summoned in 1523 and asked by the king's chief minister, Cardinal Wolsey, to provide for repayment of the loan by a subsidy at the highest rate yet levied, 4*s*. in the pound. The resultant outcry has led historians to describe the whole parliament as a sorry tale of Wolsey's tactless mismanagement.[3] Yet, as

Thomas Cromwell, a burgess in this parliament, subsequently informed a friend, the parliament in the end 'granted unto the king's highness a right large subsidy, the like whereof was never granted in this realm', and there must therefore be a suspicion that Wolsey never expected his first request to be granted in full, but was merely establishing a bargaining position. In 1512, after all, Wolsey's predecessor, Archbishop Warham, had asked the Commons for £600,000, but he had settled for £127,000.[4]

A large grant was eventually made in 1523 after serious doubts had been raised about the purpose for which the money was required—war against France—and despite the anxieties of members that it would drain the realm of cash. A Commons delegation to Wolsey first offered a smaller sum than he had initially requested, spread over two years, but the Cardinal rejected the proposal angrily, telling the delegation that he 'would rather have his tongue plucked out of his head with a pair of pincers' than accept so miserly a sum. A second visit by Wolsey to the Lower House did little to ease matters. According to the chronicler Hall, the Cardinal claimed that the realm was in fact very prosperous, and he pointed to 'sumptuous buildings, plate, rich apparel . . . fat feasts and delicate dishes'; after he left, the Commons agreed amongst themselves that 'honest apparel of the commodities of this realm, abundance of plate and honest viandes, were profitable to the realm, and not prodigal'. The Commons were still prepared to offer only 2s. in the pound on lands, or on goods worth over £20, 1s. in the pound on those with goods valued at between £2 and £20, and a poll-tax of 8d. on men over 16 assessed at short of £2. Even this had been achieved, according to one member, only after 'the greatest and sorest hold in the Lower House . . . that ever was seen . . . in any parliament', and after the knights of the king's council 'and other his servants and gentlemen' in the Commons had been over a long period 'spoken with and made to say yea, it may fortune contrary to their heart, will and conscience'.

But Wolsey was not content, and told the Commons, both untruthfully and unconstitutionally, that the Upper House had agreed to pay a higher rate. One of the court officials in the Lower House, Sir John Hussey, knight of the shire for Lincolnshire, then proposed that gentlemen worth over £50 per annum in land should grant one extra shilling in the pound, to be paid in the third year, a proposal to which ten or twelve knights present agreed, although other gentlemen were discontented and the burgesses were silent, 'for they would not condemn nor let [i.e. hinder] the gentlemen to charge themselves'. This motion, which one commentator tells us produced much ill will for its originator, was obviously intended to set a good example— Hussey was a former comptroller of the royal household, and master of the wards—but it did not satisfy anyone. After a short prorogation the 'landed' interest, finding itself burdened with an additional tax of 1s. in the pound, proposed that those with £50 a year in goods should pay the same in the following, fourth, year. A split in the Commons then developed between the 'landed' and the 'propertied' interest, the burgesses claiming that 'the motioners of this demand were enemies to the realm'. The speaker intervened, and finally, 'after long persuading and privy labouring of friends', agreement was given to the proposed fourth-year grant. The largest grant of the reign so far—£136,256 —was thus secured. However, the cost was high: so long had the various debates taken that other matters in which the Cardinal was interested, most notably the attack on enclosures, had to hold fire.[5]

If Wolsey's part in what may thus be regarded as a successful attempt to secure funds for an unpopular war is less obviously foolish than has been suggested, the role of another major figure, Thomas More, the speaker of the Commons, is clear. When he accepted the speakership More knew that a demand for a large sum of money would come before the House, since the imperial ambassadors had reported as early as March 1522 that parliament would be asked 'for the subsidies and services necessary' for the king's 'great affairs, especially the expedition against the Scots' and 'the invasion of France': the commissioners for the 1522 loan had been instructed to raise it on the security of 'such grants and contributions as shall be given and granted to his grace at his next parliament'. In agreeing to the speakership, then, More knew that one of his duties would be to steer through a royal request for aid, and aid on an unprecedented scale. Indeed, after Wolsey had made his initial request to the Commons for £800,000, it was More who repeated the Cardinal's arguments and 'enforced his demand strongly, saying that in duty men ought not to deny to pay four shillings of the pound'. Thomas Cromwell also noted that the king's careful deliberations over the war had been explained to the Commons not only by Wolsey but also 'by the recapitulation of the right worshipful best assured and discreet speaker'. The speaker's role was clearly crucial in the last stages of the debate, when much persuading and bullying went on amongst the 'king's friends'.

It is surely of great significance that after the dissolution of the parliament Wolsey himself recommended that More should be given a present of £100 in addition to the customary fee, 'which no man could better deserve . . . than he hath done'. This gift More accepted with graceful and grateful words of thanks addressed to Wolsey. Despite More's eloquent words about freedom of speech, despite his conscientious scruples about heavy taxation, in 1523 he had done, and done efficiently, what the king and the Cardinal had asked of him. Both Wolsey and Henry were aware of the debt that they owed to their helpful official. It was doubtless Wolsey who secured for More in June 1524 the High Stewardship of the University of Oxford, whilst Henry in September 1525 made him chancellor of the duchy of Lancaster.

There is therefore little in More's conduct of himself as speaker that can be regarded as advancing the power of the Commons or withstanding royal authority. Even his request for freedom of speech at the opening of parliament was less significant than has sometimes been claimed. In his address More had argued that it would be 'to the great hindrance of the common affairs' if members were not 'utterly discharged of all doubt and fear how any thing, that it should happen them to speak, should happen of [the king] to be taken' and he had begged that Henry might allow every member 'to discharge his conscience, and boldly, in every incident among us, to declare his advice'. This is, certainly, the first recorded instance of a speaker making such a plea; it is of interest that Hall found it worth noting in his *Chronicle*. However, Hall did not describe More's speech as a novelty, and it seems probable that in this instance, as so often, what at first appears like a radical new step was in truth no more than a formal recognition of an existing state of affairs. As Professor Roskell has pointed out, the advance apology made by the speaker throughout the fifteenth century for anything he might subsequently say to offend the monarch 'rested on an assumption on the Commons' part that they were liable and perhaps very likely to offend'.[6] Indeed, Roskell concludes that 'although there is no clear categorical indication that the Commons in the pre-Tudor period enjoyed free speech de jure, certainly there were times when they seem to have practised it de facto'.[7]

A close examination of the parliament of 1523 thus modifies the traditional view of Wolsey as a tactless mismanager of parliament, and perhaps also that of More as a stalwart defender of the liberties of the Commons: both Wolsey and More were crown servants, advancing the interests of their master as best they could. No obvious clash of interest existed, however, even for More: parliaments existed to serve the king, and his task as speaker was primarily to see that they served him in as efficient a manner as possible.

By the time the next parliament of Henry's reign began on 3 November 1529 the relative positions of Wolsey and More had been reversed. Wolsey had fallen from the king's favour, been stripped of his secular power, and banished from court; More had succeeded him as chancellor.

Two points need to be made about this parliament. First, no one, including the king himself, knew that it would be 'the Reformation Parliament': indeed, the term was probably not employed before 1859 and did not come into common usage until the twentieth century. The king had summoned parliament primarily to associate it with his condemnation of Wolsey, although in the event Wolsey's case was heard before King's Bench and judgement had been pronounced before parliament opened. None the less, the shadow of the Cardinal's fall lay over the assembly: the meeting began with a blistering attack by the chancellor, More, on Wolsey, whom he described as 'the great wether', and later in the session forty-four articles of complaint against Wolsey were laid before both Houses. The king doubtless also had some hope that parliament might assist him in his search for a divorce from Catherine of Aragon: certainly, Catherine herself, the imperial ambassador, and other friends believed that an attack on her was amongst the reasons for parliament's summons. The imperial ambassador and other well-informed sources thought, too, that the king intended to ask parliament for money: Chapuys wrote that the purpose of the meeting was 'to hear certain complaints against the administrators of justice and of the finances of the kingdom, in which they say much abuse and defalcation have prevailed in former times'.

What Henry's subjects in general expected of the parliament we do not know, although the plans laid by one of the great London companies, the Mercers', give us some insight.[8] The Mercers drew up a list of five proposals that they wanted laid before parliament: one asked those assembled 'to have in remembrance . . . how the king's poor subjects, principally of London, have been polled and robbed, without reason or conscience, by the ordinaries'—that is, the judges in church courts—'in probating of testaments and taking of mortuaries', but the other four proposals concerned matters of local trading interest. It appears, then, that even this well-informed and sophisticated group did not envisage any wide-ranging attack on the church.

Secondly, there were later to be many complaints about the subservience of this parliament, and the notion was put about that it was 'packed', that is, filled with the king's friends. However, such complaints were not voiced in 1529, when the meeting was first assembled, but subsequently, and were probably the result of wishful thinking on the part of those who believed that no free assembly would have been involved in processes of which they disapproved so much. (The activity of Thomas Cromwell in the by-elections of 1533 and the election of 1536 may have lent fuel to such complaints.) There were, of course, a number of 'king's men' in the Commons of 1529—we have already considered the use made of duchy of Lancaster seats—but there is no evidence to suggest that particular trouble had been taken over the elections.

None the less, the important questions about the Reformation Parliament relate to royal influence: it is not only what was achieved in this parliament that is interesting, but the means by which it was achieved. How spontaneous, for instance, was the attack on the church? How easy was it for individual members to resist the will of the king? Why did the church crumble so readily? Before we try to answer these questions, however, let us briefly review the events of these years.

According to Edward Hall, the chronicler, who had been elected as a burgess for Wenlock, the first thing the Commons did in

1529 was 'to commune of their griefs wherewith the spirituality had before time grievously oppressed them'. Complaints were expressed about mortuary fees, about priests serving as bailiffs and stewards, about their involvement in the tanning industry and the cloth trade. Sir Henry Guildford, comptroller of the king's household, apparently alleged that he and the other executors had been charged 1,000 marks for proving the will of Sir William Compton, and many others told similar anecdotes. The Commons instructed the lawyers amongst them to draw up bills dealing with mortuary, probate, pluralism, and non-residence, and these bills quickly passed the Lower House.

When the mortuary bill arrived in the Lords it was surprisingly well received—perhaps, as Hall cynically tells us, because it affected only parochial clergy and not the great spiritual peers. However, when a bill dealing with probate came before the Upper Chamber, the archbishop of Canterbury and other clerics 'frowned and grunted'. John Fisher, bishop of Rochester, made an unwise speech in which he apparently compared England to Bohemia: this enraged the Commons, for Bohemia was regarded as a near-anarchic state. Henry, who wanted the Commons to make faster progress with a bill currently under consideration releasing him from an obligation to repay his forced loan, a bill that the Lords had already passed, smoothed things over, and after a new version of the bill had been drafted, perhaps with some government assistance, the measure was passed. However, the spiritual peers were now thoroughly alarmed, and opposed to a man the bill which the Commons sent up against pluralism and non-residence. Once again Henry intervened, organizing a meeting between eight of the Commons and eight peers, which had the effect of lining the temporal peers up behind the Commons. Finally, the bill was passed after the addition of provisos so numerous that one authority has suggested that 'few priests would have felt the act's full rigour'. Despite such concessions, the clergy had come out of the session considerably mauled.

None the less, it would be an error to see this session as dominated by hostility towards the church. Of the twenty-six statutes passed, only three dealt with ecclesiastical affairs, the others being concerned with such matters as land tenure and trade.[9] Historians are unfortunately very dependent for this and some later sessions of the parliament on Hall's *Chronicle*, since no

House of Commons Journal is extant for a period before 1547. Hall's testimony needs to be treated with caution, even though he was an eyewitness, for he was perhaps more hostile to the church than many of his colleagues, being a lawyer, and thus a member of a group traditionally jealous of the privileges of the clergy; he was also associated through his position of under-sheriff with the London merchants, who considered themselves badly treated by Wolsey.

Postponed several times, the second session of the Reformation Parliament did not begin until January 1531. It was to be dominated by Henry VIII's continuing matrimonial difficulties. Summoned to Rome by Pope Clement VII in March 1530, Henry resorted to threats. These had two main thrusts. He told the pope that he would refer the divorce case to parliament, which had, he asserted, power to resolve it, and he undermined the pope's position in England by an attack on his main supporters, the clergy. In July 1530 charges of praemunire had been laid against fifteen clerics: now the whole body was forced to protect itself against such charges.

Chapuys reported on 31 January 1531 a story that the clergy in convocation had agreed to pay the king a large fine as compensation for its recognition of Wolsey as papal legate. He believed that the king was holding out to the clergy the hope that in return they might be reinstated in some of the privileges stripped from them in the previous session, and be given some more precise definition of praemunire. However, in the event the king made no such concessions, and the clergy had to agree ignominiously to a fine of £118,000. They were also forced to accept a pardon that included a recognition of the king as 'sole protector and supreme head' of the English church, although they managed to add to this a saving clause, 'as far as the law of God permits'.

However, it was the third session of the Reformation Parliament, begun on 15 January 1532 and continuing until 14 May, which finally broke the clergy's ability to resist Henry. The battle began with a bill introduced to the Lords forbidding newly appointed bishops from paying to the pope the customary annates, or first year's income. The spiritual peers opposed the bill, and the addition of a clause delaying the implementation of the measure for a year as well as the presence of large numbers of temporal peers was required to get it through. In the Lower House the unusual device of a division was necessary before the bill was passed.

The Commons themselves were meanwhile considering clerical abuses and in particular 'the cruelty of the ordinaries' in heresy proceedings. What the role was in this attack of Thomas Cromwell, who had entered the king's council the previous year, is not clear, but it seems probable that he actively assisted by producing already-prepared draft bills.[10] On 18 March the speaker presented to the king a list of abuses, shaped in the form of a petition: it complained about the legislative power of convocation as well as the unjust character of ex-officio proceedings, the use of excommunication for trivial offences, the large number of holy days, and other matters. Henry passed this on to convocation, sagely observing that as a judge it was proper for him to hear what the clergy had to say in its own defence before he pronounced judgement. Confronted with this petition, known as the Commons' Supplication against the Ordinaries, Stephen Gardiner prepared a stout defence of the legislative power of the clergy which suggested that the Commons had been induced by the 'sinister informations and importunate persuasions of evil disposed persons' to 'suppose such things to be true as be not so indeed', but the document finally sent to the king was probably more servile and apologetic. Even so, the king when passing the clergy's answer on to the Commons on 30 April dismissed it as 'very slender'. On 10 May, Henry put three demands before the clergy: that convocation should renounce its authority to make canons without royal licence, that it should submit its existing canons to the scrutiny of a group of parliament-men and clerics nominated by him, abandoning all canons that this body found offensive, and, finally, that it should recognize the need for the king's assent for the retention of any canons. To increase the pressure on convocation, Henry sent for the speaker and a group from the Commons and informed them that the clergy 'be but half our subjects . . . for all the prelates at their consecration make an oath to the pope, clean contrary to the oath that they make to us, so that they seem to be his subjects and not ours'. The speaker returned to the Commons, where the oaths were read out, to the surprise and shock of the whole house, according to Hall.

Convocation was now in an impossible position. After debates, votes, and a visit from leading members of the privy council, it finally agreed on 15 May to the king's articles.

The clergy had been savaged. Two days after the end of the session More resigned. More's resignation was, of course, a symptom of his growing anxiety about the king's policy towards the church, but he had none the less been prepared throughout the parliament to do his duty in other areas of government. For instance, when the Commons were asked for a grant of taxation, it was More who explained to them that a subsidy was needed to strengthen the Scottish borders, an assertion that unfortunately, although predictably, led to discussion of the incontestable proposition that friendship abroad was better than even excellent fortifications. Thomas Temys, member for Westbury, then boldly suggested that if the king took back Catherine there would be no danger of foreign intervention. Although, in the end, the question of taxation was not pursued, it is clear that, on the public stage at least. More was the king's loyal servant throughout the session: his anxieties and doubts about the divorce and the policy adopted by Henry towards the church did not prevent him from fulfilling his official functions.

By the time of the opening of the fourth session of parliament, in February 1533, major changes had taken place in Henry's private circumstances. In January 1533 he at last married Anne Boleyn, who was already expecting a baby. To secure the succession for this child, and to prevent controversy about the validity of the marriage, it was essential to prevent intervention by the pope. Cromwell's answer to the problem was a bill which cut off all appeals to Rome, making it possible for ecclesiastical authorities within England to render a final decision in the king's case. (The appointment of Cranmer as successor to Warham in early 1533 ensured that such a decision would be in the king's favour.) The appeals bill came before the Commons on 14 March, when it was criticized by some merchants, who were worried that if the king were to be excommunicated the emperor and other Catholic princes would impose a trade embargo: one of the members for London apparently went so far as to offer the king a grant of £200,000 if he would remit his case to a general council. However, other members of the Commons argued that many foreign

princes were favourable to what the king was doing, and by the
time of the prorogation on 7 April the bill had been passed
without significant alteration. At a later date Sir George
Throckmorton was to claim that in a conversation with Sir
Thomas Dingley the latter had declared himself surprised at the
ease with which the appeals bill had passed; Throckmorton had
replied cynically that few men wished to displease the lord privy
seal. However, the passing of this important act perhaps owes
less to Cromwell's bullying than to the care which had been taken
over its drafting and the attraction, particularly to the lawyers in
the House, of its claim that 'in divers sundry old authentic stories
and chronicles it is manifestly declared and expressed that this
realm of England is an empire, and so hath been accepted in the
world'.

Four days after the prorogation Cranmer petitioned the king
for permission to judge the validity of his marriage to Catherine
of Aragon. On 23 May the archbishop declared the marriage
invalid, and five days later he pronounced the union with Anne
Boleyn lawful. Anne was crowned queen on 1 June. Thus, the
royal matrimonial problems that had first caused the break with
Rome appeared settled. The consequences of the break, however, were to preoccupy parliament for many years to come.

The fifth session of the parliament, which took place in the
early spring of 1534, witnessed a further attack on the financial
relationship between England and the papacy. The Commons
passed a bill to transfer the payment of annates, threatened by the
1532 statute, from the pope to the king. The measure ran into
trouble in the Lords, where the original bill was dropped and a
new one introduced. Although this bill was passed, it merely
suppressed annates, and did not transfer them to the king, as
Cromwell had originally intended. However, over other monet-
ary tributes to the pope, such as Peter's pence (originally an
annual payment from every householder possessing land of over
a certain value, but fixed since the twelfth century at £200 p.a.),
Cromwell easily obtained his desire, which was merely their
abolition.

Another important religious measure passed in this session
confirmed the submission of the clergy and repeated the demand
of a draft Cromwell had prepared two years earlier for reform of

the canon law. Finally, a bill introduced into the Lords on
21 February attainted Elizabeth Barton, the so-called Nun of
Kent. Both Fisher and More were endangered by the attack on
Elizabeth Barton, but the Upper Chamber apparently showed so
much hesitation about condemning the former lord chancellor
that his name was not included amongst those said to have
listened to the Nun's dangerous prophecies. (Fisher was able to
secure his pardon by a payment of £300.)

A major preoccupation of the government remained the succession. As early as 1533 Cromwell had realized that settling the
succession would involve the reducing of Catherine to the position of Prince Arthur's widow, and a bill to this effect appeared
before the Lords on 11 February 1534. Despite Chapuys's best
endeavours the bill passed both Houses without great difficulty
—the ambassador had asked Henry if he might go before parliament to explain Catherine's position, but the king sought refuge
in the argument that it was not the custom for foreigners to
appear before the assembly. Perhaps because of the continuing
negotiations with the Scots, which involved the Scottish claim to
the English throne, the bill ratifying Henry's marriage to Anne
Boleyn did not appear before the Lords until 20 March. It was a
carefully drafted proposal, in which Cromwell's suggestion that
speaking or writing against the marriage should be termed
treason had already been reduced by other councillors to misprision of treason. By it, the succession was vested in Anne's
heirs: neither the Princess Mary nor the Scottish line was mentioned. All subjects were required to swear an oath affirming the
'whole effects and contents' of the act, and subjects imperilling
the king by deed or written word were henceforth to be deemed
traitors.

The sixth session of the Reformation Parliament, which began on
3 November 1534, passed what was perhaps the most permanently significant piece of legislation of this parliament relating to
the English church—the act of supremacy: the monarch was now
to be regarded as 'the only supreme head in earth of the Church of
England'. First fruits and tenths were also annexed to the crown:
every new incumbent of a benefice would pay his first year's
income to the crown, and the monarch would in future also
receive one-tenth of the annual value of the benefice. The act also

sanctioned the setting up of a commission to ascertain the value of all spiritual preferments, a provision which was to produce the famous Valor Ecclesiasticus. Surprisingly, this bill apparently did not encounter opposition, even in the Lords, perhaps because the king sweetened the blow by a remission of one-fifth of the payment of £118,000 with which the clergy had bought their pardon in 1531.

To fill a gap which had been discovered in the succession statute passed in the previous session, an act was now framed establishing a definite oath of obedience to the king and his heirs, whilst another act made it high treason maliciously to 'wish, will, or desire, by words or in writing', harm to Henry, Anne, or their heirs. Under this act, which created a new statutory offence of treason by words, More, Fisher, and the Carthusians were to die. According to Fisher's brother, Robert, who was one of the members for Rochester, 'there was never such a sticking at the passing of any act in the Lower House as was at the passing of the same . . . for now . . . speaking is made high treason, which was never heard of before'. Although there is little contemporary evidence to support Fisher's story of opposition to the bill, it gains credence by the decision of Protector Somerset's government in the first parliament of the next reign to repeal the statute as one of the over-cumbersome winter clothes that could be cast off in the summer of the boy-king's reign.

Cromwell had other concerns in this session besides the succession, however. One of the most pressing of these was money, and he therefore introduced a bill granting the king two subsidies, a fifteenth and a tenth. There appears to have been, astonishingly, no opposition to the bill, despite the fact that it abandoned the traditional assumption that the monarch could ask for 'extraordinary revenues'—that is, taxation—only in 'extraordinary circumstances', by which was meant, essentially, war. The remainder of the time the monarch was expected to live off his 'ordinary revenues', that is, his income from crown lands and feudal dues.

In 1534 England was at peace, and the making of a grant of taxation in such circumstances has led Sir Geoffrey Elton to suggest that here, and in the subsidy act of 1540, Cromwell introduced a new principle that justified taxation in times of peace: the preamble to the 1534 act, he has pointed out, refers to the king's services to the country, and that of the 1540 act to the nation's 'wealth, surety, and quietness' under Henry's beneficial rule.[11] Elton's argument can be further supported by the fact that in 1545, when the foreign situation was in truth very threatening, the preamble to the subsidy act referred primarily to the advantages the realm had received from the good government of the king, and concluded by requesting him to accept the grant 'as it pleased the great king Alexander to receive thankfully the cup of water from a poor man by the highway side': although the grant could have been justified in terms of military necessity, it was not.

However, Elton's arguments have been attacked, most notably by Gerald Harriss.[12] Mr Harriss drew attention to the fact that although the 1534 act does indeed emphasize the quiet and unity of the country it also mentions the need to subdue the Irish rebellion and the 'defence of this his majesty's realm'. Similarly, the 1540 act lists as reasons why the grant was made the expense of fortifying Calais, Berwick, and Carlisle, and the cost of suppressing the Pilgrimage of Grace.

Mr Harriss has undoubtedly undermined Elton's claim for the novelty of the 1534 and 1540 subsidy acts. None the less, he does not entirely overthrow it. A vital item of evidence in support of Sir Geoffrey's view is the 1553 subsidy act, passed in the second of Edward VI's parliaments, a subsidy requested and granted in time of peace. Whilst the dangerous foreign situation was mentioned in the act, the grant was couched largely in terms of the gratitude that the realm owed the king for his godly rule, and the need to pay his debts. There is far more emphasis on these than there is on military or defensive needs. The next subsidy act, that of 1555, is even more striking. It again was a grant made in time of peace, and on this occasion not even a fleeting reference was made to military needs in the preamble. The grant was justified solely in terms of 'the great and sundry benefits which we have many ways received at their majesties' most gracious hands' and also mentions the crown's debts. Moreover, although there certainly was opposition to this grant, the fact that it was being requested in peacetime and without even a pretence that defence needs were particularly pressing does not seem to have been mentioned.

Thus, the subsidy act of 1534 undoubtedly marked a change in the nation's perception of how government was to be financed, even though, as we shall see, those in parliament were reluctant to acknowledge this change openly (see below, pp. 121–2).

Although it had been intended that parliament should reassemble on 3 November 1535 an outbreak of plague in London delayed the seventh session until 4 February 1536. In early March a bill was introduced in the Lords to confiscate the estates of monasteries yielding less than £200 p.a.—these were equated with communities consisting of less than twelve persons. According to Thomas Dorset, vicar of one of the City churches, the king himself appeared when the bill was read in the Commons, which suggests that the government had some doubts about the reception the bill would receive, but in the event neither House seems to have regarded it with great hostility. One reason for this was that an extensive programme had been undertaken to prove that the small monasteries were, as the preamble to the act declares, full of 'vicous, carnal and abhominable living'. Hall reports that the abbots in the Lords were prepared to see small monasteries go if by that sacrifice they could save their own houses, 'but even at that time one said in the Parliament House that these were as thorns, but the great abbots were putrified old oaks and they must needs follow'.

Another reason for the ease of the bill's passage may have been that members had already perceived that the measure might be personally beneficial. An informant told Lord Lisle on 3 March that it was rumoured 'that abbeys and priories under iij c marks by years, and having not xij in convent shall down', but Lisle appears to have been alerted even earlier, for on 22 February one of Thomas Cromwell's servants informed him that he had received Lisle's request for the abbey of Bewley but did not expect 'that the same or any like' would be suppressed during the current session. Before the end of the session at least five peers had asked for a share in the spoils. So had two members of the Commons, Sir John Neville and Sir Peter Edgcombe.

But lay landowners did not have it all their own way in this session, for another statute vastly increased the dues paid to the king on the death of his tenants. From about 1300 the casual side-effects of feudal tenure had become more valuable than the regular services to which lords were entitled. These feudal 'incidents', or irregular payments—fines on the alienation of land, 'reliefs' when an heir entered into his inheritance, and so on—become well worth exploiting. They were particularly important to the king, the greatest of the feudal landlords. However, since feudal incidents were burdensome, lawyers had constantly attempted to arrange their clients' property in such a way as to attract the least amount of incidental taxation, and in particular, inheritance duties. One method of doing this was through the use, a procedure by which lands were held by a continuing group of trustees to the use or profit of another: land never descended to an heir, and feudal incidents could therefore be avoided. A use was also a means by which landowners could escape the tyranny of the legal rule of succession, providing for younger sons, daughters, and the rest. By 1500 it was claimed that the greater part of the land of England was held in use, and the king was obviously losing a great deal of revenue.

Henry VII made one or two minor alterations to the law, but it was his son who fully revived 'fiscal feudalism'. In 1529 he persuaded a number of notables to sign an agreement which permitted evasion on two-thirds of an estate in return for recognition of an inescapable obligation on the other third. This agreement was not apparently laid before parliament immediately, but in 1532 Thomas Cromwell produced a draft bill which probably raised the obligation to one-half of an estate. This increased demand was an error: Hall reported that the Commons would have agreed to the proposal if the king had been less greedy, but, as it was, 'strange words' were used against the king and his councillors. Cromwell thought about the matter again in early 1534, but what expedited action was the decision that same year of the master of the rolls and the judges in the Dacre case. Lord Dacre had died in 1533, leaving all his considerable estate tied up in such a way as to rob the king of his feudal rights. Dacre's arrangements were set aside by the judges, who were probably jealous of the growth in chancery power caused by the use. Faced with the possibility of all such arrangements being over-turned by the courts, and doubt being cast on a great many titles to land, parliament was forced in 1536 to accept a statute which recognized uses, but declared that persons profiting from them were to be subject to feudal incidents; the statute also denied landowners the right to devise their land at will.

By this statute the crown restored feudal incidents for socage tenants as well as for tenants by knight service, and it reimposed compulsory primogeniture. The measure was naturally much disliked and it was to be complained about in the Pilgrimage of Grace. In 1540, therefore, a compromise not unlike the draft of 1529 emerged in the statute of wills, which freed two-thirds of land held by knight service from feudal incidents, and conferred the legal right to dispose of freeholds by will.

No eyewitness account of the dissolution of this momentous parliament exists. But contemporaries were not unaware of the importance of what had happened. Amongst the demands of the Pilgrimage of Grace, for instance, were a number that related to parliament: the pilgrims wanted further representation for the North, reform of the election of knights of the shire and bur-gesses, and 'the use among the lords in the parliament house after their ancient customs'. Above all, they wanted a new parliament to meet, either at Nottingham or at York, 'and that shortly'. What had been done by parliament, they recognized miserably, had to be undone by parliament.

Thus, England had been divided from Rome, the succession altered, the lesser monasteries dissolved. The treason law had been extended, and the power of the monarch increased over a whole range of affairs. How had this been possible?

First, and most important, many of those who sat in parlia-ment agreed with what the king was doing. One did not have to be a rabid religious radical to dislike the intervention of a foreign bishop in English church life, or to feel that the church's financial resources would be better used for the education of the parish clergy than for the maintenance of a number of inefficient mon-astic houses. Resentment of clerical privilege obviously also played some part in producing support for Henry's actions: the traditional 'anticlericalism' of some groups well represented in parliament, merchants and lawyers, could be exploited by Thomas Cromwell. Another problem for the clergy was the long-standing enmity of the lay peers, jealous of their spiritual brothers' privileges. In the third session of the parliament, for example, it was the lay peers who forced the bill in conditional restraint of annates through the Upper House with only the earl of Arundel amongst their number opposing it.

Secondly, as we have seen, the preoccupations of contemporaries, and their interest in parliamentary affairs, were not necessarily those of subsequent historians. Historians concentrate on debates touching religion, the constitution, and the succession, but it is not clear that they were the things of most importance to the majority of those who sat in sixteenth-century parliaments, or to those who observed them. In March 1534, for example, John Grenville wrote to his master, Lord Lisle, in Calais, telling him, quite erroneously, that 'Sir Thomas More is clearly discharged of his trouble', and enclosing copies of the new treason and supremacy statutes; quite half of the letter, however, is concerned not with these weighty matters but with a sensational story about a female prisoner's escape from the Tower.

Thirdly, and perhaps most important, few of Henry's subjects, including those in parliament, saw the statutes passed in this parliament as the beginning of 'the Reformation'. They could be viewed either as a long-overdue rationalization of church organization, or as another round in the centuries-long dispute between popes and monarchs over control of the church, but they did not mark any substantial shift away from orthodox doctrine. Many of those who supported the royal supremacy were, like Stephen Gardiner, to be horrified when in the next reign they discovered that it might be the route whereby Protestantism was introduced into the English church.

But it is also important to remember that those few men who did oppose royal policies in parliament had a hard task. Amongst the many advantages enjoyed by the government was the fact that it alone knew what policies it intended to implement, and it could therefore organize a propaganda campaign accordingly. In addition to books for a general audience, the government circulated works aimed specifically at those in parliament. A number of writings against the pope were distributed before the parliament's fifth session, for example: John Rokewood described in March 1534 how 'daily doctors and great clerks maketh new books and writeth [against] his pomp and other his inordinate living'. There was a similar propaganda effort, this time against both the doctrine of purgatory and the smaller monasteries, before the seventh session; indeed, on 7 February 1536 Chapuys reported that a pamphlet had been printed 'for the information' of members 'containing a list of the measures to be discussed therein'.

Additionally, a number of procedural manœuvres were available to the crown in the Chamber. Of these the most important was the division, used perhaps for the first time in the Commons in 1532 to secure the passage of the bill for the conditional restraint of annates: Chapuys tells us that Henry 'caused the house to divide, and some passed to his side for fear of his indignation'. Few were brave enough to stand out publicly against the king's will, and those who might have done so were often silenced by government tactics.

The government also took pains in these years with membership of and attendance at parliament: indeed, it is perhaps in the Reformation Parliament that the by-election appears for the first time. Before the fourth session of 1533 Cromwell ensured that vacancies in the ranks of the Commons were filled; two knights of the shire were elected, for example, to occupy the places left in Essex by Audley's elevation to the chancellorship and the death of Thomas Bonham. Cromwell also improved the position of the government in the Upper House by the admission of the abbot of Burton and the eldest sons of the earls of Wiltshire, Arundel, and Shrewsbury. Before the fifth session of January 1534 Cromwell made notes of those members who had died since the last meeting, presumably with an eye to filling their places, and he told those members of the Lords whom he feared might disagree with his policy that their attendance could be dispensed with. Meanwhile the king was trying by gentler means to win over principal members of the Commons. Before the sixth session Roger Wigston wrote to Thomas Cromwell about a vacancy in Warwickshire caused by the death of Sir Edward Ferrers, telling him that 'secret labour is made among the freeholders against the coming down of the writ. As it is your mind to have the house furnished with good and discreet men, I shall be glad to learn your pleasure.' Attempts to secure a pliant assembly were also made at the seventh session of February 1536, and Cromwell further instructed Henry 'to grant few licences for any to be absent from the parliament'. It was rumoured that abbots were forbidden to attend the meeting, and a number of churchmen and peers opposed to the king's policy certainly did not come.

Even without such intervention the church might have found defending its position difficult. The traditionally low attendance rates of the spiritual peers ensured that, for example, in the vitally important session of 1534 no more than twelve heads of religious houses were ever present, and only between four and six bishops; by contrast, sometimes as many as thirty-eight temporal peers attended. Only three monastic clergy are known to have attended the seventh session of the parliament, which decided upon the fate of the smaller monastic houses. The church at this period did not, or could not, marshal its forces in the face of an unprecedented attack.

Still, despite such difficulties, there was criticism of the monarch, and opposition to his policies in the Reformation Parliament. The best-documented example is that of Sir George Throckmorton, knight of the shire for Warwickshire. Throckmorton seems to have been a persistant irritant in the flesh of Thomas Cromwell, and in 1536, after he had shown an unwise interest in the demands of the Pilgrimage of Grace, the secretary had him interrogated about his conduct during the previous years. Throckmorton then declared that even before the Reformation Parliament had met he had been summoned by Catherine of Aragon's confessor, William Peto, who had advised him, 'as [he] would have [his] soul saved', to oppose the Boleyn marriage. Throckmorton also said that after he had spoken in the Commons against the act in restraint of appeals, he was praised by Bishop Fisher and two other conservative clerics, Nicholas Wilson and Richard Reynolds, who told him that although he need not persevere with such speeches if they seemed to have no effect, his good example might be of value to others. Throckmorton was undoubtedly courageous, for when, as a result either of this speech or of some other, he was summoned before the king, he repeated what Father Peto had told him of Henry's sexual relations with Anne Boleyn's sister and her mother. Henry was rather taken aback by this, managing only to reply feebly that he had not had carnal relations with Anne's mother. Nor with her sister, interposed Cromwell firmly. It was too good a story not to be repeated, and Throckmorton appears to have told Sir William Barentyne, knight of the shire for Oxfordshire, and Sir William Essex, knight for Berkshire, what had been said.

Throckmorton, Barentyne, Essex—who was arrested with Throckmorton in 1536—Sir Marmaduke Constable, knight of the shire for Yorkshire, and Sir John Giffard, who sat for Staffordshire, were in the habit of meeting in the Queen's Head

Tavern in Fleet Street to discuss parliamentary affairs. If there was an opposition group in the Reformation Parliament Throckmorton and his friends formed its core. However, they were outmanœuvred by Cromwell, by whom, as Throckmorton admitted, 'the Common House was much advertised' so that 'few men would displease him'. Throckmorton himself promised the secretary in late 1533 that he would 'stay at home and meddle little with politics'. Constable also stayed away from the next session of parliament.

It has sometimes been suggested that this group worked in collusion with the more famous critics of Henry's policy, Fisher and More. When he was questioned in 1536 Throckmorton certainly told his interrogators that he had been encouraged in his stand not only by the clerics, but also by More himself, who had sent for him and told him that if he continued 'in the same way' and was not afraid, he would 'deserve great reward of God'. There are problems about this story, since it appears to relate to the period when the bill of appeals was under discussion, a time at which More was residing quietly at home in Chelsea rather than lurking in the parliament chamber. None the less, we may accept that Throckmorton, whose sense of chronology was shaky, on some occasion received comforting and encouraging words from More about his criticisms of royal policy. However, this is the only evidence for any link between More and the parliamentary opposition of the 1530s. If the critics of the crown were being in any sense 'orchestrated', the orchestrating was done by Peto and by the imperial ambassador, Chapuys, not by More.

In any case, the crown's critics in this parliament were totally outmanœuvred by Cromwell. He devoted far more attention to parliament and its management than any minister had done before him, worrying about attendance and by-elections, drawing up lists of members for various purposes, bullying, threatening, and doubtless also praising. That this meeting is so significant in the history of parliament as well as that of the church is undeniably due in large measure to these efforts.

5

Mid-Tudor Parliaments

The consequences of the Reformation Parliament were immense, for parliament as well as for the religious history of England. Because Henry VIII had used parliament in his fight with the pope, his son was to use it to carry through a Protestant reformation: because the Reformation had been sanctioned by parliament, the Counter-Reformation of Mary's reign had also to be carried out through parliament. Of course parliament had concerned itself about religious matters before the Reformation, but the Reformation and the changes of the subsequent decades, changes carried out by statutory authority, brought parliament into the centre of religious debate to an unprecedented extent: Hooker's treatise on parliament of about 1571 would indeed declare that the chief justification for parliament's existence was the need to see 'that God be honoured'.

This central role was recognized by clergy and laity alike. In 1547 the lower house of convocation asked that the lesser clergy might be represented in the Commons—the bishops, of course, already sat in the Lords—so that 'such statutes and ordinances as shall be made concerning all matters of religion and causes ecclesiastical may not pass without the sight and assent of the said clergy'. Although the lower clergy had in fact been summoned to parliament in the early fourteenth century, their request for a return to 'the ancient custom of this realm' was not granted. The anxieties of the lower clergy were justified, however, for although individual bishops appear to have been consulted, convocation was not shown either the 1549 Prayer Book or its successor of 1552.

It was thus to parliament that those who wanted religious change applied themselves. The martyrologist John Foxe in Mary's reign addressed his petition against the revival of the act of six articles to the parliament, and it was to parliament that the Puritans later sent their *First* and *Second Admonitions*. Parliament's position was, for the time being at least, secure therefore: after a period of insignificance in the later fifteenth and early sixteenth centuries it was once again playing a central role in the nation's affairs.

Religion

All the major religious changes of these years were promulgated through statute: it was by statute that the two Edwardian prayer books were sanctioned, and by a parliamentary statute that England was reunited with Rome in 1554. (Protector Somerset did, however, toy briefly with the idea of altering religion 'by the king's authority' alone, but obviously decided in the end that the changes he envisaged needed the greater force that statute would provide.[1]) In 1554 Cardinal Pole tried desperately to prevent the pope's agreement that Englishmen could keep their former church property being included in the statute whereby England was reunited with Rome, but the view of the lawyers that property rights could be fully protected only by statute prevailed.

However, by no means all those who sat in parliament appear to have been interested in religious matters. Indifference and lack of understanding are the background to many of the measures passed in this period. They explain, for example, the history of the 1539 act of six articles, a measure reinforcing belief in transubstantiation and the giving of communion to the laity in one kind only. There was criticism of the crown's proposals in the Lords by Shaxton, bishop of Salisbury, but in the Commons there was little opposition other than that of Thomas Broke, member for Calais. Broke, who subsequently spent some years in prison on the suspicion of heresy, made a long speech in which he described the doctrine of transubstantiation as 'a gross and foolish error'. Although Broke was supported by at least one fellow member, the chronicler Edward Hall, who asked that the scriptural arguments in favour of transubstantiation should be set out at length, most of the House were soon 'weary' of the subject. A letter to Lord Lisle, governor of Calais, tells how the comptroller of the king's household, Sir William Kingston, taunted Broke 'so much that it is unlikely that he will ever speak of it again': what Kingston seems to have said is that if Broke were to make the same points after 12 July, the day on which the act was to come into force, then he, Kingston, would be ready personally to bring a faggot with which to burn him. What emerges from this story is the very limited support that religious radicalism had in the Lower House, and the unwillingness of most members to be involved in theological controversy.

This general indifference in doctrinal matters on the part of the Commons can be further illustrated from the reign of Edward, a reign in which the doctrine of the English church was dramatically changed through statute. Only twice did the House of Commons raise any substantial protest against government policy. The first occasion on which the Commons put difficulties in the way of an Edwardian religious bill was over the 1547 proposal for the dissolution of the chantries. This statute was necessary because an act passed in 1545 allowing Henry to dissolve them had lapsed with his death. Interestingly, the 1545 statute had itself not had an easy passage in the Commons— at the end of the session secretary Petre reported that 'the book of colleges etc escaped narrowly, and was driven even to the last hour, and yet then, passed only by a division of this House'— but we know nothing of the grounds on which the objectors stood.

It is clear, however, that when the Edwardian bill ran into difficulties in 1547 the opposition to it in the Commons was not primarily religious. A first draft, passed by the Lords, was dashed in the Commons, probably because it would have dissolved all lay corporations and craft guilds: thus, livery companies and the like would have disappeared. A second bill, drafted by one of the king's serjeants, carefully excluded lay corporations and guilds, but none the less also ran into problems. The chief opponents in the Commons of this second bill were the representatives of King's Lynn and Coventry, who, according to the privy council register, 'incensed many others to hold with them'. Privy councillors interviewed the burgesses and discovered that they were chiefly concerned about the fact that at King's Lynn the income from chantries was used to maintain the town pier, whilst at Coventry, a town that had once been rich but was now decayed, the income was used to maintain the fabric of its churches. One obvious answer to these problems would have been a proviso to the general bill protecting the interests of the two boroughs, but the councillors were anxious lest this should 'have ministered occasion to others to have laboured for the like'. The burgesses for Lynn and Coventry were therefore persuaded 'to desist from further speaking or labouring' against the bill by a promise that the interests of their towns would subsequently be safeguarded by letters patent, which were in fact granted in May and December 1548. The bill then passed.

Unlike the Henrician act, which justified the dissolution of the chantries in almost entirely secular terms, the Edwardian act argued that masses for the dead are doctrinally incorrect; it also, unlike the earlier measure, made some provision for preachers, schoolmasters, and poor relief. Although Professor Scarisbrick declares that the bill was 'rail-roaded through' and implies that the financial concerns of the Coventry and King's Lynn burgesses were somehow a cover for other and higher considerations, there is in fact no evidence that the reasons given by the burgesses for their opposition were anything other than the truth.[2] The whole story is better regarded as an illustration of the way in which crown and parliament tried to reconcile their occasionally conflicting interests.

The second occasion in Edward's reign on which the Commons opposed a government religious bill was in 1552, when a measure came from the Lords that would have deprived the conservative Tunstall of the bishopric of Durham on the grounds of misprision of treason. Members of the Lower House asked for the personal appearance of the bishop before them to discuss the charges; the government apparently took fright, dropped the bill, and subsequently deprived Tunstall by commission. The fact that both Lord Stourton and the far from conservative Cranmer opposed the bill in the Lords suggests that the reason why the Commons were sympathetic to Tunstall may have been unrelated to his religious views: it was perhaps dislike of what was seen as a proposal of dubious legality that prompted the Commons.

The picture that thus emerges in Edward's reign is of a malleable House of Commons, anxious about threats to material interests—for instance, in the chantries bill—but less concerned, and less interested, in matters of dogma. The House of Lords was, of course, a different matter, for there conservative bishops and lay peers fought every change from the 1547 bill for the administration of the sacrament in two kinds to the 1552 bill for clerical marriage: the 1549 act that 'laymen, having wives, may be priests and have benefices', for instance, was opposed in the Lords by eight bishops and four lay peers.

At first glance the picture looks very different in the reign of Mary. The standard view of what happened in parliament in Mary's reign, based on Notestein and Neale, is that Protestant, independent-minded gentlemen in the House of Commons then caused the government considerable problems. Notestein argued that 'there appeared in the Commons something almost like a protestant party which yielded ground only as it was again and again out-voted', whilst Neale declared that though brief, Mary Tudor's reign marked

a stage in [their] apprenticeship to future greatness . . . the queen's policy was unpopular with many of the politically articulate gentry . . . there was a degree of organisation about the parliamentary opposition in 1555 which, although in some ways a flash in the pan, marks a significant stage in the evolution of the House of Commons.[3]

However, it can easily be shown that Neale both overestimated the strength of this opposition and saw it as more Protestant than it actually was. The first of Mary's parliaments, that of October 1553, restored religion to its 1547 state. From 20 December 1553 religious services were to be conducted and the sacraments administered as they had been in the last year of Henry VIII's reign. This important measure produced, it is true, some trouble in the Commons, but no formal division was reported, suggesting that those who opposed the bill were considerably in the minority. Bishop Gardiner declared that 'out of 350 votes only 80 had gone against', and these not 'men of importance'; this figure, if correct, suggests that those who opposed the bill amounted to no more than just over one-fifth of the Commons.

In the next parliament, that of April 1554, a proposal to revive the medieval heresy laws, laws which authorized the burning of heretics, was defeated. Can this be seen as evidence to support Neale's theories? Probably not, since the bill was defeated not in the Commons but in the Lords, where the secular peers' dislike for any increase in the power of the bishops seems to have been crucial: the peers concerned later claimed that they had been persuaded that the bill's object was 'to give the bishops authority to treat them vindictively'. The peers said that 'they had not intended to favour heretics or heresy', and their claim is substantiated by their willingness six months later in Mary's third parliament to pass an apparently identical measure. Personal rivalries at court, an anxiety about the future of secularized church property, and antagonism towards the bishops: these, and not Protestantism, are what explains the defeat of the heresy bill.

In Mary's third parliament, begun in November 1554, England was reunited with Rome. The passage of the bill making this possible was slow, but the reason for the delay was continuing anxiety about church land rather than hostility to the reunion itself. Cardinal Pole, who had been received in parliament by both Houses on their knees, asking tearfully for forgiveness, fought long and hard to prevent the pope's dispensation for the holders of former ecclesiastical property being included in the bill itself, since he believed that to include it amounted to simony. In the end he was defeated, and the bill then passed without difficulty. Only one member of the Lower House, Sir Ralph Bagnall, spoke against it, and his anxieties were not about doctrine but about an oath he had taken against the pope in the reign of Henry VIII, a king whom he much admired. His colleagues, many of whom had taken the same oath, merely laughed at him.

The best-known of Mary's parliaments is that of 1555. In 1555, according to the Venetian ambassador, the House of Commons was 'quite full of gentry and nobility, for the most part suspected in the matter of religion, and . . . more daring and licentious than former houses, which consisted of burgesses and plebeians'. Far too much has been built on this casual remark by a man who was new to the country and who could not speak English. As we have seen, from at least the early fifteenth century the Commons contained a high proportion of gentlemen; this was no sudden innovation of 1555. None the less, the fact remains that the House of Commons was daring and licentious, for it opposed two bills desired by the queen. One of these was the bill restoring to the church the first fruits and tenths annexed by Henry VIII. This bill was finally passed by crown supporters keeping the House sitting until the unusually late hour of 3 p.m., when, presumably, members critical of the proposal had given up and gone to lunch. The other bill that caused trouble, the exiles bill, would have permitted the monarch to seize the lands of Englishmen who had gone abroad and refused to return. The bill was defeated by a violent incident in which Sir Anthony Kingston, knight of the shire for Gloucestershire, locked the doors of the Chamber and forced the speaker to put the bill to the vote before he had time to rally its supporters.

Did this daring and licentiousness originate from Protestant-ism? Certainly the annexation of first fruits had been one of the opening moves of the Henrician reformation, and many of the exiles who would have been affected by the second bill had gone abroad to avoid Mary's Catholicism. But at the heart of both proposals was property, and property was something about which members of parliament cared deeply. Members might well therefore have disliked the first-fruits bill because it reduced the income of the crown and therefore increased the likelihood of burdensome taxation. Indeed, in this same parliament the queen asked for a grant of taxation, and the tactless juxtaposition of this demand with the proposal for the return of first fruits may explain much of the opposition aroused. Crown interference with property was regarded with particularly great suspicion, as the discussions over attainder and treason bills show, and members may have disliked the exiles bill primarily because it undermined security of tenure: why should men lose their lands for doing something—living abroad—which was in no way illegal? Any member of this parliament may have disliked the exiles bill on the grounds of an attack on property rights without having any sympathy for the religious sentiments of the exiles.

Thus, it seems as if the notion that the House of Commons in Mary's reign grew in organizational skills under the direction of Protestant-minded gentlemen has to be abandoned. The evid-ence for opposition to the queen's policies on doctrinal grounds is very slight, and that for anxiety about property rights very considerable. This is not surprising when we remember that the Marian government had tacitly permitted Protestants in a posi-tion to do so to leave the country: criticism of Mary's religious policy, although always an irritation, was a great deal less of a nuisance to the government when voiced in Geneva than it would have been in the House of Commons.

The events of these years suggest that parliament had come only slowly to understand its new role as an arbiter of doctrine; after all, the common lawyer Christopher St German was in the mid

1530s still asserting that statute was void if it offended against the law of God, an argument used by Sir Thomas More at his trial. Although by Elizabeth's reign Thomas Egerton was prepared to declare that 'though an act of parliament pass without [convocation's] consent, yet it is firm and good', it seems probable that many of those in parliament, and, in particular perhaps, those in the Lower House, understood the force of Bishop Scot's argument in 1559 that parliament should not meddle with matters of faith and religion, since it consisted

for the most part of the noble men of the realm, and certain of the commons, being lay and temporal men, which although they be of good wisdom and learning, yet not so studied nor exercised in the scriptures, the holy doctors and practice of the church as to be accounted judges in such matters.

Although some of those in parliament had gradually come to believe that they could interpret the wishes of the Almighty without the advice of convocation and the bishops, many of the Commons clearly remained hesitant and uncertain, willing to follow the lead of the monarch and his advisers, whatever that lead might be.

Economic and Social Matters

However, the resurgence in parliament's importance was not confined to matters of religion. The 1530s and 1540s witnessed attempts by both theorists and men of affairs to analyse the ills of England and suggest ways in which they might be remedied, and the way in which many of them sought to improve things was by statute. There thus came into being the humanistic concept of a brave new world created by parliamentary activity. A document of about 1531 associated with Christopher St German, for instance, not only argued that parliament should take various steps to improve the church but also presented the case for public works as a means of providing employment for the poor. A little later John Rastell, More's radical brother-in-law, wanted bills to be drawn up dealing with the reform of common law and chancery, with clerical marriage and the abolition of prayers for the dead. In 1542 Henry Brinkelow's *Complaint of Roderick Mors unto the Parliament House of England* suggested various worthy purposes to which confiscated church property could be put, including the establishment of hospitals. *Piers Plowman's Exhortation unto the Lords, Knights and Burgesses of the Parliament House*, addressed to the second session of Edward's first parliament, demanded statutes to convert wasteland to arable or pasture, to remove the restrictions on corn exports, and to protect home manufactures by the imposition of duties on imported goods. Another pamphlet of the same date, *An information and petition against the oppressors of the poor commons of this realm, compiled and printed for this only purpose, that amongst them that have to do in the parliament, some godly-minded men may hereat take occasion to speak more in the matter than the author was able to write*, argued that amongst 'the manifold and most weighty matters' to be discussed in parliament, the most serious was the plight of the poor.

Because of these men, and because of the increasing desire of government to regulate economic and social life, statute came to control more and more aspects of life: acts were passed in the sixteenth century regulating wages, establishing standards of quality, enforcing apprenticeship, and protecting industries. Bills were introduced into the Reformation Parliament to regulate traders as diverse as saddlers and pewterers. In 1540, the House of Commons passed bills dealing with bakers and with brewers, with coal and with firewood. Members of the Commons were also concerned about agricultural problems, and with town planning: it was in the 1530s and 1540s that a number of towns secured statutes enabling them to rebuild decaying property. It has been calculated, indeed, that three-quarters of the statutes passed in the later parliaments of Henry VIII dealt with economic and social matters.[4]

The zeal of those who wished to reform through statute becomes clear if we consider a major social problem of the period, poverty. Parliament had passed a statute against vagrancy in 1531, which decreed that unlicensed beggars should be whipped. In 1536 a more radical statute attempted to set up some form of public employment for beggars, and to organize collections for the impotent poor. This lapsed at the next parliament, and in 1539 Thomas Cromwell thought about introducing a new measure, but in the end did not do so. In 1547 a draconian statute allowed for the enslavement of beggars. This act was clearly unsatisfactory, and parliament repealed it in 1550, restoring many of the provisions of the 1531 act. A statute of 1552 instituted a system of voluntary weekly contributions towards the upkeep of the poor, and this was repeated in another statute of 1555, which also included a recognition of the Catholic emphasis on personal acts of charity. The 1555 act was followed by another in 1563, and so on (see below pp. 116–17).

As problems became acute, so the government and the property-owning classes looked to parliament to solve them. The late 1540s and 1550s, for example, saw a crop of statutes that were a response to rising food prices. Thus an act of 1550–1 against the enclosure of commons and waste permitted settlement on waste of up to three acres per cottage, and reinforced the medieval statute of Merton, whilst another in 1552 decreed that land which had been under the plough for four years since 1509 should be returned to tillage, although fields used for certain crops such as saffron, hops, flax, and madder were exempted. A statute was passed in late 1554 forbidding the export of corn and a number of other commodities after prices had risen above a certain level, and a year later another statute attempted to encourage more tillage. Those who attempted to act together in response to economic conditions were dealt with by a statute in 1548–9 against victuallers who fixed prices and workmen who conspired to fix wages. In the next session of parliament, after the rebellions of 1549, a bill was read for the punishment of unlawful assemblies. This proposal, which began, interestingly, in the House of Lords, had a difficult passage which included six readings and other debate; the act made it treasonable for twelve or more persons to assemble together to murder or imprison a member of the privy council, or for forty or more to break down enclosures etc.

One consequence of all this activity was to make it more and more desirable to sit in parliament and keep an eye on what was going on. By so doing, men could protect or even advance their businesses, trades, or localities. This was the more necessary because within a single trade or industry there could of course exist very diverse interests, all of them seeking legislation. A clear example of this is the leather industry, which took up a great deal of parliamentary time in the 1550s, when conflict raged between the tanners and the curers; another, more obviously, is the cloth industry, where not only did the interests of the weavers have to be weighed against those of spinners, and the interest of the seller against that of the buyer, but consideration also had to be given to the varied needs of different regions—for example, a bill was read in 1547 to regulate cloth-making in East Anglia, in 1555 an act was passed for cloth-making in Worcester, and another for Bridgwater cloths, and in 1559 an act was passed for cloth-making in Essex.

Trades and industries began to organize themselves, not only to put forward certain proposals in parliament, but also to resist those that they did not care for. 'Lobbies' of weavers, kersey-makers, and fishmongers sprang up, and the corporation of London even found it necessary in the 1500s to discourage too many members of the leather industry from trying to influence what went on in the House.

Matters of State

None the less, the person to whom parliament mattered the most remained the monarch. Parliamentary consent was necessary, of course, for the granting of taxation. In 1549 Somerset's government even attempted a radical new approach to taxation, with the introduction of a tax on sheep. This tax, which used to be regarded as a means of reducing the size of flocks and thereby relieving rural unemployment, is now generally recognized as an attempt to restore to the crown the large income from wool and cloth which it had received in earlier centuries. However, provisos added to the bill in the House of Commons reduced its fiscal impact, the tax was much disliked in the West, and it was repealed a year later. Northumberland and Mary reverted to more traditional methods. In 1555, however, the monarch's request for a subsidy and three fifteenths ran into difficulties in the Commons, where members claimed that the grant would be a burden on 'the poor and needy'. Clearly one factor in the opposition to the request was the juxtaposition of a demand for parliamentary taxation with the bill restoring first fruits and tenths to the church. To demand taxation as the same time as surrendering voluntarily a part of the royal income—causing, as some members noted, 'infinite loss to her majesty and but little profit to others'—was obviously tactless. Another reason for the difficulty Mary encountered was a feeling in the Commons that 'there is not lack of means for relieving the queen without burdening the people': she should, members argued, 'compel all the debtors of the crown to pay up their arrears, there being no one, or but a few, of the great personages . . . who do not owe some five, some six, some eight thousand pounds sterling and upwards'. In the end, nevertheless, the queen was granted a subsidy and two fifteenths.

Parliament had also become of central importance in matters relating to the succession. The parliament of 1536, after all, had been summoned specifically to deal with the crisis arising from Henry VIII's rejection of Anne Boleyn, and the assembly was to play a vital role in establishing the succession 'in such wise as all ambiguities, questions and arguments thereof may be extinguished'. Parliament again played an important part in 1540 when Henry wished to secure a divorce from Anne of Cleves: the two Houses held a meeting to consider the matter, and sent a delegation to see the king. In 1543, however, another succession act apparently reduced parliament's role by allowing Henry to leave the crown to whomsoever he chose in his will.

Many of these parliaments also considered other matters relating to the succession, such as the acts of attainder whereby those who seemed to threaten the crown were destroyed. From his earlier sparingness with such acts, Henry came in the 1530s to use them very extensively: one single act of 1539, for example, contained fifty-three names, and in the parliamentary session of 1540 there were five acts of attainder, including that of Thomas Cromwell himself. Cromwell was condemned to death by parliamentary statute alone: he had no opportunity to defend himself in a court of law. Most of the people attainted in the later years of Henry's reign were equally unfortunate; although it was not necessarily Cromwell who began this process of substituting legislation for a common law trial, he certainly used it extensively, and it is perhaps not unjust that he was destroyed by a weapon he had used so freely.

Although parliament played no part in the manœuvres which placed Edward Seymour in control of the realm after Henry's death, nor in his fall in October 1549, both his career and that of his younger brother, Thomas Seymour, provide evidence of the continuing importance of parliament as an arena for political infighting. Thomas Seymour was bitterly jealous of his brother's pre-eminence, and seems to have regarded parliament as the means by which he could acquire some of the power to which he thought he was entitled. He is said, for instance, to have opposed in 1547 both the act repealing Henry VIII's treason legislation and the act which repealed a Henrician statute enabling Edward at the age of 24 to revoke by letters patent the statutes passed during his minority. Seymour's behaviour became worse and wilder, and in early 1549 he was attainted and executed. The act of attainder claimed that he had tried to gain control of the young king and generally ferment trouble, a plan that failed, because Edward, although bribed with extra pocket-money, refused to co-operate.

The interest of Seymour's actions for us is that he was not only planning a coup, he was obviously planning a parliamentary coup. The charges laid against him on 17 January 1549 claimed that Seymour had written a letter for the king to sign, with which he had then 'determined to have come into the Common House himself and there with [his] favourers and adherents before prepared to have made a broil or tumult and uproar'. This claim was almost certainly true. Seymour had told Lords Clinton and Dorset that he intended 'to put a bill into the parliament houses . . . which I pray you grant me your consent unto and get me as many of your friends in the house as you can', and he had asked Rutland before the session whether he would take his place in the Lords, saying that he hoped he would, 'for that he trusted to have' his voice. Seymour had also made lists of members of the Lords whom he thought would be persuaded to favour him.

Did this parliamentary coup stand any chance of success? Seymour seems to have had a number of friends in the House of Lords, even if some of them, like Rutland, were later persuaded to testify against him. His position in the Commons, however, was even stronger, partly because of the considerable patronage he could wield through stewardships and territorial possessions. William Wightman, his secretary, sat for Midhurst. At Bramber, a barony owned by Seymour, his close associate William Sharington was returned; Sharington, the under-treasurer of the Bristol mint, was himself attainted in early March 1549 after a trial at Guildhall, although he was not in fact executed. Seymour had further patronage through his position as lord admiral: for instance, it was to him that Sir Francis Fleming, who sat for Lyme Regis, owed his position as lieutenant-general of ordnance.

Through his wife, the former queen, Catherine Parr, Seymour had links with her servant William Smethwick, who sat for Penryn; with her auditor, Anthony Bouchier, who sat for his own borough of Shoreham; with Nicholas Throckmorton, sewer of the queen's chamber, who was returned for Devizes; with Andrew Bainton and John Vaughan, who sat for Horsham, part of the barony of Bramber; with Francis Goldsmith, another of Catherine's servants, who sat for Chippenham; John Cock, general receiver of the queen's revenues and Seymour's steward, who was apparently returned for both Cardiff and Calne; Robert Warner, sewer of the queen's chamber; and Clement Throckmorton, her cup-bearer. There was, then, a hard core of Seymour's associates in the Lower House, and there were enough of them to make his plans feasible.

Certainly the care with which the council handled the attainder bill makes it clear that trouble was anticipated in parliament. The council had agreed that 'parliament should have the determination and order of the case', but it also decided that before the bill was introduced members of the council who sat in either the Upper or the Lower House should interview Seymour, so that 'neither excuse for him nor information to the House should want if he would or could make any answer or defence'. The chancellor, Warwick, Shrewsbury, Southampton, Baker (the speaker of the Commons), Cheyne, Smith, and Deny therefore interrogated Seymour. By the end of February 1549 the bill had passed the Lords, but it was difficult to get through the Commons. According to the privy council register, the bill was 'very much debated and argued' in the Lower House. The House asked to see the evidence of Seymour's guilt, and treated the case against him with grave suspicion. Finally, the bill was passed in a full house. However, despite the efforts of the government, and the intervention of the speaker and various privy councillors, ten or twelve members are known to have voted against it.

Seymour was immediately executed. Even then, the government was uneasy, and seems to have undertaken an extensive propaganda campaign—for example, Latimer in his sermons declared that Seymour was a man 'the furthest from the fear of god that ever I knew or heard of in England' and 'a covetous man, a covetous man, indeed . . . an ambitious man . . . a seditious man, a condemner of common prayer'. On 5 April Latimer found it necessary to justify the fact that Seymour, like Cromwell, had been condemned by parliament without being seen: a man that answers for himself at the bar is

not allowed his man of law to answer for him, but he must answer himself. Yet in the parliament, although he were not there himself, any friend he had, had liberty to answer for him, frank and free . . . the tenor of the writs in this—every man to speak the best he knoweth of his conscience, to the king's majesty's honour and the wealth of the realm . . . there were in the parliament, in both Houses, a great many learned men, conscionable men, wise men. When that man was attainted there . . . they had liberty to say nay to his attainment if they would.

Somerset's power did not long survive his brother's fall. His fellow councillors stripped him of his authority in October 1549, and in January 1550 articles against him were laid before the Upper House, where the peers insisted on satisfying themselves that his confession had not been 'forced'. Somerset was soon released from the Tower, however, and even restored to the council. But not for long. In the autumn of 1550 there were rumours that he was hoping for a meeting of parliament, to which he would explain, it was said, how the people were 'oppressed with fresh taxes', and 'those in power governed simply after their own caprice, without respecting the laws and customs of the realm'. In late 1551 Somerset was finally charged with plotting against his colleagues, and indicted under both the 1547 treason act and the 1550 act that made it treasonable to assemble troops with the purpose of murdering or imprisoning a privy councillor. As a peer, he was entitled to a trial before the high steward's court. Cleared of treason, but convicted of felony under a clause of the 1550 act which referred to the bringing together of men for a riot, Somerset was executed on 22 January 1552. It is surely of great significance that parliament did not reassemble until the following day.

Northumberland, in this as in so many other things, learnt from Somerset, and took great trouble with parliament. In October 1551, for instance, the chancellor was asked to find out what members had died since the last meeting 'to the intent that grave and wise men might be elected to supply their places, for the avoiding of the disorder that hath been noted in sundry young men and others of small judgement'. The government took an active interest in the consequent by-elections. The sheriff of

Hertfordshire was instructed 'to use the matter . . . as Mr Sadler may be elected and returned' to replace the deceased Sir Henry Parker, but in this instance the council's nominee was not chosen. In Surrey, too, where the council had sent a writ for the election of a knight of the shire, accompanied by an instruction to the sheriff to 'prefer' Sir Thomas Saunders, the council's instructions were ignored. In March 1553, before Edward's second parliament, very considerable pains were taken over the elections: the council put forward nominations in Hampshire, Suffolk, Bedfordshire, Surrey, Cambridgeshire, Berkshire, Oxfordshire, and Northamptonshire. The duke was also interested in the composition of the Upper House, asking Cecil whether it was possible to summon the heirs apparent of certain peers by writ, 'only upon the grace and favour of his majesty'. His own son and two others were accordingly summoned. Northumberland was not simply concerned about who was to appear in parliament: he was also anxious to arrange business in the manner most satisfactory to the crown. In December 1552, for instance, he wrote to the council about what should be discussed in the forthcoming meeting, arguing that members should be told that the crown's debts were largely the fault of Henry VIII and 'the wilfull government' of Somerset. During his brief period of power Northumberland thus showed himself as anxious to control parliament as either Thomas Cromwell or William Cecil.

The coup after Edward's death, like its more successful predecessors, took place outside parliament. However, this was a necessity forced upon Northumberland by the sudden worsening of Edward's illness, for it had initially been intended that the diversion of the succession to Lady Jane Grey should be sanctioned by parliament. Parliament had indeed been intended to meet on 18 September 1553, and chancery had begun to draw up the writs before Edward's death forced the duke's hand.

The accession of a woman raised many constitutional uncertainties, and had the effect of thrusting parliament once more into the centre of efforts to settle the succession. One of the first statutes of Mary's reign declared the marriage between Henry VIII and Catherine of Aragon valid. As well as the assertion that 'truth, being of her own nature of a most excellent virtue, efficacy, force and working, cannot but by process of time break out and show herself', the statute contained much malice about Cranmer, and a claim that God had shown his displeasure in earlier years by sending plagues and rebellion. Perhaps encouraged by this recognition of parliament's role, the House of Commons on 16 November sent a deputation to the queen. Through their speaker, the Commons implored Mary to marry and settle the succession, but asked her not to ally with a foreigner, since that would be financially disastrous and might lead to a succession struggle. Foreigners, the speaker declared, would 'wish to lord it over the English'. Mary, who had secretly pledged herself on 29 October to marry Philip, was very cross: 'parliament was not accustomed to use such language to the kings of England', she said, 'nor was it suitable or respectful that it should do so'. Ten days later, on 26 November, the first moves were taken towards what we know as Wyatt's rebellion; four members of the Commons as well as a number of peers were involved. The formal announcement that Mary would marry Philip was postponed until the day after parliament had been dissolved.

   The next parliament of the reign, meeting in the aftermath of the rebellion, was in part taken up by the inevitable acts of attainder. But it also witnessed a major departure from precedent, for Mary's marriage treaty with Philip, in which he relinquished all claim to the disposal of offices in England and agreed to observe the laws of the realm, was turned into a statute. This was in part a fulfilment of Mary's promise in the Guildhall at the height of the rebellion that she would marry only with the consent of the realm, but the break with tradition none the less makes it clear how anomalous was the position of the king consort. Statute was therefore frequently called upon to deal with such matters as the signing of official documents and the extension of the treason laws to cover a situation not dreamt of in 1352. Mary's third parliament, which began in November 1554, was particularly exercised over the question of how the country was to be governed were Mary to die bearing the child with which she was thought to be pregnant. The measure finally passed decreed that Philip should be the guardian of a female heir until she reached the age of 15, and a male one until he was 18; moreover, during the minority, Philip was to have control of the kingdom as well as of the person of his child. However, to Philip's chagrin, the restrictive provisions of the marriage treaty were to remain in force during the minority, a provision which perhaps explains why the English had insisted on the treaty being turned into a statute.

At the end of this parliament, the crown took the unusual step of instituting legal proceedings against 106 members who had left early without obtaining the speaker's permission. The eighteenth-century historian John Strype suggested that there was a political motive behind these persecutions, and others have argued that the members left because they disliked the legislation reuniting England with Rome. This last seems extremely improbable, since there are amongst them a number of men of proven devotion to the Catholic Church, such as the lawyer Edmund Plowden.[5] More recently, Michael Graves has argued that the men who left were staging a protest against the bill dealing with the guardianship of the heir.[6] Following a report by the imperial ambassador that the earls of Arundel, Pembroke, Westmorland, and Cumberland had also absented themselves in order 'not to give their consent to a measure infringing upon the right hitherto exercised by the nobility to appoint a protector when need has arisen', Graves linked the departures from the Commons with those of nine peers whom he believes stayed away from parliament in order to avoid giving their consent to the bill. But this entire argument rests on the premiss that the bill, in its final form, was favourable to Philip, which, as we have seen, it was not. Moreover, those who were opposed to the bill were still in the Commons, amending and altering it, on 12 January 1555, the date on which the absentees were formally noted as not being present: the bill did not pass the Lower House until 14 January.

Whilst it is not impossible that there was some political motive behind the absence of those peers mentioned by Renard—after all, a bill extending to Philip the protection of the treason laws had had a difficult time only six months earlier—it is worth noting that most of them had attendance records below average: it may be unwise to make too much of their absence on a particular day. There is no convincing evidence of links between the members of the Commons who left early and the absentee peers. The relative political inexperience of many of those involved, the proximity of Christmas, the wish to travel in company suggested by the fact that thirty-six of them left with their fellow members: these are surely the explanations for a level of absenteeism which was by no means unusual in the sixteenth century (see above, pp. 40–1). It is the decision of the crown to proceed against those who had ignored the express command of 22 December 1554 that no one should 'depart into their country [i.e. county] this Christmas, nor before the parliament was ended' which is remarkable, not the absence of the members. However, in the event, only twenty-five of those indicted were fined.

By far the most controversial aspect of Philip's position, as far as parliament was concerned, was the matter of his coronation. Philip and his advisers seem to have believed, for reasons that are not altogether clear, that the coronation was particularly significant in England as a confirmation and recognition of title. The imperial party therefore constantly urged Mary to secure her consort's coronation. However, both they and Mary herself seem to have felt that Philip could not be crowned without the consent of parliament, and this was never forthcoming. Indeed, parliament was so clearly averse to the scheme that no formal proposal was ever laid before it. Mary thus recognized that there were certain principles of the constitution that she could not overturn, and that parliament was the guardian of those principles. In a quite different way from that of her sister, Mary's problems over marriage and the succession thus helped to secure parliament's place in political and constitutional life.

6

Elizabethan Parliaments

The 1559 Church Settlement

The first parliament of Elizabeth's reign began on 25 January 1559 with a service in Westminster Abbey. Historians have scrutinized with care the form taken by that service in an attempt to understand Elizabeth's intentions, but the episode, like so many of those involving Elizabeth, is shrouded in ambiguity. When the queen met the abbot of Westminster at the door, 'robed pontifically, with all his monks in procession, each of them having a lighted torch in his hand', she declared, 'Away with these torches, for we see very well', a comment which has led some writers to suggest that Elizabeth disliked all the monks' popish ceremonial. However, she apparently accepted the incense and holy water with which she was also greeted, balking only at the processional lights.[1] This middle position fits Elizabeth's declaration to Philip II's envoy, Count Feria, that she was resolved 'to restore religion as her father left it': the implication was that although she needed to resume the supremacy, without which her claim to the throne itself was shaky, she hoped to avoid doctrinal change.

Not until 9 February was a bill read in parliament 'to restore the supremacy of the church in England, etc to the crown of the realm'. The history of this bill, which was replaced on 21 February by a different version drafted by the Commons, is one of the great unsolved mysteries of sixteenth-century parliamentary history. We do not know what the government intended, we do not have drafts of the various stages through which the bill went, and we know little about the motives of those involved.

Until recently the most convincing theory has been that put forward by Sir John Neale in *Elizabeth I and her Parliaments, 1559–1581*, published in 1953. Neale argued that the original intention of the inherently conservative queen had been to introduce into her first parliament only a bill restoring the royal supremacy, leaving the doctrine and ceremonies of the church otherwise untouched. He suggested that Elizabeth's plans were altered by the House of Commons itself, a House which was dominated, he thought, by religious radicals. These radicals, according to Neale, forced Elizabeth to accept a uniformity statute as well as an act of supremacy, and, moreover, a uniformity statute which authorized the use not merely of a Protestant prayer book but of the radical 1552 book.

Since Neale wrote it has become clear that he greatly exaggerated both the numbers and the coherence of the radicals in the House. He believed, for instance, that there were in the Commons at least twelve and probably sixteen returned exiles, men whom he described as 'wolves', so voracious were they in their desire to see true Protestantism established in England. Subsequent research has shown that there were, in fact, nineteen exiles in the House in 1559, but that they did not form the cohesive group envisaged by Neale, partly at least because many of them had not in fact been 'exiles for religion'. Sir Ralph Bagnall, for instance, who sat for Newcastle under Lyme, had gone to France to escape his creditors. Sir Edward Rogers, Elizabeth's vice-chamberlain, if he went abroad at all—and there is some doubt about this—went to escape punishment after Wyatt's rebellion. Even Francis Walsingham, later to be 'the hotter sort of protestant', seems to have travelled in Europe in Mary's reign for largely academic reasons, studying law at the highly regarded University of Padua alongside Sir Henry Neville, who was knight of the shire for Berkshire, John Astley, and Sir Thomas Wroth. There is no reason to believe that even amongst the returned exiles there was a universal desire to see a Calvinist church in England: indeed, only one of the 212 individuals registered with the English church at Geneva sat in the parliament of 1559, and his identification is shaky.

Some historians, aware of this weakness in Neale's explanation of the evolution of the 1559 church settlement, have tried to demolish it entirely. Winthrop S. Hudson, for example, argued that Elizabeth's own religious views were firmly Protestant, and that she had always intended that her first parliament should give statutory authority to a prayer book as well as to an act of supremacy.[2] Norman L. Jones has taken a similar line:[3] Elizabeth, he declares, 'was as protestant as Jewel, Grindal or Cox'. Dr Jones believes that Elizabeth always intended to have an act of uniformity as well as an act of supremacy, and that the uniformity that she wanted was that of the 1552 book.

All this is, in the final analysis, incapable of firm proof. Whoever was in fact behind the various drafts of the supremacy bill, and whatever it contained by the time that it got to the House of Lords, it was there stripped of almost all meaning. Even so, nine bishops, the abbot of Westminster, the earl of Shrewsbury, and Lord Montagu voted against it. On 22 March the bill, amended and considerably altered by the Lords, came back to the Commons, and was reluctantly passed there. Two days later the parliament was prorogued for the Easter recess.

During the recess there was, as Neale hinted, a struggle at court. We do not know much about it, but those involved clearly included Francis Russell, second earl of Bedford, the student and correspondent of many Continental Protestant divines, including Calvin, who made 'an abusive attack' on the Holy See in parliament, describing it as 'a sink of crime and a cess-pool of iniquity'. Others involved were the lord keeper, Nicholas Bacon; the chancellor of the duchy of Lancaster, Sir Ambrose Cave; Robert Dudley; and, above all, Cecil. It was Cecil who later said of the religious settlement, 'I must confess I am thereof guilty'; in 1574 Thomas Sampson wrote reminding him 'what you did, and could do, in the beginning of the reign . . . what your authority, credit, and doing then was, you know, God knoweth, and there are many witnesses of the same'.

On 10 April a new supremacy bill was read in the Lower House. On 26 April the bill received its final reading in the Lords and was passed there, but passed with all the bishops registering a protest, as well as the abbot of Westminster and Lord Montagu. By this act, Elizabeth became 'Supreme Governor' of the Church of England: the title 'Supreme Head' had been jettisoned, perhaps, as Jewel reported, because Elizabeth herself believed that 'this honour is due to Christ alone, and cannot belong to any human being whatsoever', perhaps because of Catholic susceptibilities.

Not until 18 April was a uniformity bill introduced in the Commons. It was passed in the Lords on 28 April by twenty-one votes, with the bishops and lords Shrewsbury, Winchester,

Montagu, Morley, Stafford, Dudley, Wharton, Rich, and North all voting against it. This act sanctioned the use of the 1552 Prayer Book, but in a toned-down version, with the words of institution taken from the more ambiguous 1549 book, and no 'black rubric'.[4] Moreover, the 'ornaments of the church and of the ministers therefor' were also to be those of Edward's second year, before the radicals had stripped the church of most of its medieval decoration.

By these two acts, the English church was once more separated from Rome, and rendered doctrinally Protestant. It seems highly improbable that this settlement was what Elizabeth had intended. Certainly her subsequent actions suggest little sympathy for the 1559 settlement. By the statute of uniformity the queen was empowered to promulgate 'further ceremonies and rites' if she so wished, and a month after the end of parliament, Elizabeth authorized a set of injunctions. These were conservative in tone. For instance, except at the time of communion, the holy table was to stand in the chancel, and the communion bread was not to be the same as that used normally at dinner, despite what the 1552 Prayer Book had decreed. The Latin Prayer Book authorized by the queen in 1560 for college chapels and private use was even more conservative, frequently reverting to the uses of the 1549 Prayer Book, including reservation of the sacrament for the sick, and requiems. When we add all this to Elizabeth's insistence on the use of a crucifix in the chapel royal and her dislike of married clergy, it becomes difficult to accept the arguments of Hudson and Jones about Elizabeth's Protestantism.

That the settlement was even what the majority of those in parliament really wanted is also uncertain. The conservatives were of course leaderless, owing to the death of Cardinal Pole, and the bishops and laity in any case disunited over the issue of church lands and the problem of leases made by bishops whose right to their episcopal position was subsequently challenged.[5] Convocation, itself apparently drifting rudderless, had done nothing to assist the conservatives in parliament, and, indeed, by its confirmation of the authority of the pope made their position more difficult. But the really decisive event of these weeks was the stand against the royal supremacy taken by the Marian bishops in the Lords. When they all voted on 18 March against the royal supremacy, they dashed any chance of restoring the late

Henrician church, despite the fact that this was probably what Elizabeth and a sizeable number of her subjects wanted. In order to secure the supremacy and her throne, Elizabeth would have to purge the Marian bench of bishops, and this forced her into a dependence on more radical churchmen. The bishops' vote thus left her vulnerable to the persuasions of the Protestants at court: to Cecil, Bedford, and the rest.

Puritanism

This interpretation of 1559 obviously raises doubts about the traditional portrayal of parliament in Elizabeth's reign as the stage for mighty clashes between the queen and her Puritan subjects, battles won by Elizabeth only because of the force of her personality and the strength of her subjects' loyalty. The nature of the evidence customarily used for this portrayal has itself tended to overemphasize the role of religious dispute in the life of parliament. Because the Commons Journal for the period is very defective—the section for 1584–1601 disappeared in the seventeenth century—the historian is forced to use the collections of the seventeenth-century antiquarian Simonds D'Ewes, and the fragments of contemporary diaries that have survived. D'Ewes (1602–50) was a great amasser of materials, but his own interests were clearly Puritan and partisan—he was a member of the Long Parliament. His work, moreover, was not published until 1682, and then by his nephew. The diaries, too, obviously reflect the interests of their often anonymous writers, some of whom were far from impartial. The anonymous diarist of the 1593 parliament, for instance, was extremely interested in the doings of Sir Peter Wentworth, and certainly prejudiced in favour of the religious radicals. When describing the course of the bills against Protestant sectaries he records only hostile speeches; in fact, the majority of the House obviously favoured the bill, since it passed, and someone must therefore have spoken in its favour.

Neale and other parliamentary historians compounded the difficulties of their source material by a somewhat suspect handling of some pieces of evidence. A good illustration of this is the 'Puritan choir', a group of extremists whom Neale believed dominated Elizabeth's early parliaments.[6] The very existence of this group turns on a single piece of contemporary evidence, a satirical poem about the parliament of 1566. This poem mentions the Wentworth brothers, James Dalton, William Fleetwood, Robert Bell, Christopher Yelverton, and many others, but it does not on examination contain any evidence of Puritan convictions amongst these men, whose religious views seem in fact to have been very varied: five even had strong links with Catholicism. Sir Geoffrey Elton has suggested that the poem provides a list of the members of the Commons who served on the committee for the settling of the succession;[7] although this cannot be proved conclusively, it is clear that Neale's interpretation of the poem and its significance is erroneous.

Michael Graves's careful examination of the career of one of the 'choir', Thomas Norton, whom Neale believed to be a leader of the group. has revealed a much more complicated picture than Neale painted.[8] Norton was certainly, like many of his fellow members, concerned about abuses in the church. In both 1566 and 1571 he introduced bills for reform of the canon law, and he wrote the introduction to the 1571 edition of Cranmer's *Reformatio Legum* (printed by Foxe). But Norton was also anxious about a whole range of other problems, from the decay of Bristol trade to usury and iron mills. He was a great House of Commons man, serving, according to Graves, on 107 committees. Well regarded by members of the government, who relied upon him to assist the passage of government bills, Norton was described by the queen after his death as 'a most faithful and loyal servant to her, and such a one as had done many good services'—not the epitaph that she would have pronounced on a hostile critic.

Norton was not a Puritan. He summed up his own religious position in 1572 when he said about the claims of the *Admonition to the Parliament* that 'it is one thing to mislike the state and doctrine of our church, as they [Presbyterians] do, and another to dislike the corrupt ministration of justice, and evil executing of the laws as they be, which is the fault of men, and may without slander of our church . . . be reformed'. This is not the declaration of a radical committed to fundamental change: Norton wanted to purge the church of its abuses, but he did not wish to change its doctrines or its organization. His distinction between a concern about abuses in the church and a desire radically to restructure it is an important one. A large part of the Commons was, like Norton, interested in the reform of abuses: on the last day of the

1581 meeting, for example, the speaker told the queen that the House was concerned about 'the admitting of unlearned and insufficient ministers', 'the abuse of excommunication used in things of small moment', 'the commutacion of penance into money even in the greatest offences', and 'the great inconveniences grown by reason of pluralities and dispensations'. Most members wanted the reform of abuses such as simony, and most desired a better-educated, preaching, clergy; only a small number wanted anything more radical. The radical group—men like Job Throckmorton, Peter Turner, and George Carleton—produced a number of proposals, from Strickland's plan to reform the Prayer Book in 1571 to Anthony Cope's bill and book of 1587, but the only reform measures to receive a sympathetic hearing from the House were the moderate ones. What the majority liked was the 1576 petition against unlearned clergy. This was presented to the queen by the Lords and eventually led to convocation's drawing up of reforming canons dealing with the education of the lower clergy and the regulation of ordination. In 1584, to take another example, the Commons listened sympathetically to the plight of the ejected ministers, but when Peter Turner attempted to introduce the Genevan liturgy and book of discipline the House gave him a cold reception.

As Puritanism grew more extreme, with the publication of the Marprelate tracts and the spread of Presbyterianism, so the Commons became more cautious. By 1593, the House was prepared to pass a bill against Protestant sectaries, the Brownists. The parliament of 1597 saw a return to the kind of anticlericalism so characteristic of Henry VIII's reign, with the introduction of bills concerned with abuses in the granting of marriage licences, and against excessive fees in church courts. Even these failed. One reason for the waning of support for the reform of abuses was that such support had often been associated with fears about Catholicism and anxiety about the succession—this was clearly the case for Thomas Norton in 1571. When concern about the Catholics and the succession died down in the 1590s, sympathy for even moderate reform also diminished.

True 'Puritanism' thus achieved little in Elizabeth's parliaments. The 1559 settlement remained largely intact, despite its inconsistencies and the attacks aimed at it from right and left. Moderate proposals were more sympathetically received, partly, no doubt, because many of them had influential backing. The church hierarchy itself often shared members' anxieties: in 1566, for instance, both archbishops, and thirteen bishops, supported a proposal to confirm the reforming articles passed by convocation three years before. It was Grindal, bishop of London, who drafted a bill introduced in 1571 to compel quarterly attendance at church, a bill which passed both Houses before being vetoed by the queen. The bishops tried again in 1576 and 1581, but again failed.

Several privy councillors were also sympathetic to reform proposals: Mildmay, Walsingham, and even Burghley himself were criticized by the queen for their willingness to consider the problem of ecclesiastical abuses. In 1593 a councillor, Sir Francis Knollys, was one of the few members to support James Morice in his attack on the ex-officio oath. Knollys here went further than was usual, but most proposals for reform could expect support from individual members of the privy council.

But despite this weighty support, proposals for anything more radical than, for instance, improvements in clerical education stood little chance of success in the Commons. However, it has sometimes been claimed that, although unsuccessful in its attempts to alter the church, Puritanism made a significant contribution to the development of the tactics and organization of opposition in parliament. This is an argument difficult to substantiate for Elizabeth's reign. Puritanism made no novel use of parliament as an opportunity for publicity, for example, since, as we have seen, petitions addressed to parliament had flourished in the 1530s and 1540s. Moreover, the 1572 *Admonition to the Parliament* appeared too late in the session to be really effective. What about Puritan influence in elections? In 1586 the Dedham classis urged John Field to 'note' all the parliamentary boroughs in the county and to try to secure the return of men of favourable religious views. No evidence exists to show that Field and his friends took this advice, and certainly there is nothing to suggest that if they did so they were successful. Neale believed that the 1586 election at Warwick turned on the issue of Puritanism, since one of the candidates, Job Throckmorton, was an ardent supporter of that cause, but Derek Hirst has shown convincingly that the contest arose out of endemic jockeying for position between the principal burgesses and the lower ranks; he points out that

Throckmorton's chief supporter in the town, one Richard Brooks, was later censured for never going to church or listening to the sermon.[9]

Religious fervour does nevertheless appear to have had some impact on the behaviour of certain members, leading them to organize meetings outside the Chamber, meetings intended to sort out how they should conduct themselves inside the Chamber. In 1586 and early 1587, for example, Wentworth, Lewknor, Hurleston, Bainbridge, and Cope met and discussed the introduction of the reform proposals known as 'Cope's bill and book'. Here, then, was some degree of organization. However, it must not be too readily assumed that this was very different from what Sir George Throckmorton and his friends had been planning in the Queen's Head tavern in the early 1530s (see above, pp. 76–7). It was certainly no more successful: they all finished up in the Tower.

The incident none the less draws attention to a danger posed by religious radicalism in the Lower House: it provoked considerable and often heated discussion of the royal prerogative. By the royal prerogative was meant the rights and privileges that the ruler enjoyed over and above those of his subjects. Such rights and privileges belonged to the monarch as 'the preserver, nourisher and defender of all the people', and it was accepted that they could not be encroached upon or diminished by statute. However, whether such rights and privileges might even be discussed in parliament was a more controversial question. Elizabeth clearly believed that parliament should not even mention matters that touched upon the prerogative without her permission; those in parliament frequently took a different view, arguing that the purpose of a meeting of parliament was to express the grievances of the subjects.

Moreover, Elizabeth included amongst 'prerogative matters' topics which her predecessors had not. Many areas that touched on royal finance came, as we shall see, under this heading, but Elizabeth also regarded any criticism of the church of which she was head as an attack on the royal prerogative. This led her into some perilous seas. In 1571, for example, when one of her councillors tried to prevent the Commons from discussing the state of the church, by a declaration that 'for us to meddle with things of her prerogative, it were not expedient', the Commons would not listen and embarked on a lengthy debate, which culminated in Walter Strickland's introduction of a bill to reform the Prayer Book. Strickland was summoned before the council and sequestered the House, that is, forbidden to attend. When the House asked why he had been taken from them, Knollys replied evasively that he was 'in no sort stayed for any words or speech of him in that place uttered, but for the exhibiting of the bill into the House against the prerogative of the queen'. In the course of the consequent discussion Sir Nicholas Arnold 'moved care to be had for the liberties of the House', whilst Christopher Yelverton declared that 'the precedent was perilous'. Under 'so gracious a prince', he went on, there was no danger, but 'the times might be altered'; it was fit 'princes to have their prerogative but yet the same to be [con]strained within reasonable limits'. Finally Fleetwood suggested a way out of the crisis: 'the only and whole help of the House for ease of their grief in this case', he said, was to be 'humble suitors to her Majesty, and neither to send for him, nor demand him of right'. Strickland was restored to the House the following day.

Over Strickland, Elizabeth had been forced to retreat, and throughout the 1570s she had to fight hard to maintain her ruling that matters ecclesiastical should not be discussed in the Commons without her explicit approval, or that of her bishops. In 1572, for instance, she commanded that 'from henceforth no bills concerning religion shall be preferred or received into this House, unless the same should be first considered and liked by the clergy'. Despite this warning, religious bills were introduced, and when they were later handed over to the queen, she 'seemed utterly to mislike of the . . . bill, and of him that brought the same into the House'. In 1576 a similar attempt to prohibit debate caused Peter Wentworth to compose his great defence of the liberties of the House. 'Free speech and conscience in this place', he declared, 'are granted by a special law as that without the which the prince and state cannot be preserved or maintained.' He went on to argue that 'the accepting of such messages and taking of them in good part doth highly offend God'. Wentworth was prevented from delivering the entire speech, questioned by a committee, and finally committed 'a close prisoner to the Tower', where he stayed for a month.

The struggle continued in the next decade. In 1581 some

members delivered articles for reform of discipline in the church on the lines already discussed in 1576. The House agreed that the bishops should be asked to press the queen for reform. The queen's reply when Sandys, archbishop of York, spoke to her on the subject was that she was 'sufficient of herself to deal with the clergy in matters ecclesiastical', and that parliament 'should not meddle therein'. This reply, Sandys reported, was 'much disliked of'. After Archbishop Whitgift's attempted purge of radical ministers in 1584, petitions from Lincolnshire, Warwickshire, and Essex were presented to the Commons, complaining of the state of the ministry. The queen tried to silence discussion by pressure from the Lords at a conference of the two Houses, but failed. The speaker was summoned, and told of Elizabeth's amazement that her command 'not to meddle with these matters of rites and discipline of the church' had been ignored. The Commons responded by passing a bill to punish unlearned clergy with imprisonment.

In 1587 the speaker reported, 'you are commanded by her Majesty to take heed none care be given or time afforded the wearisome solicitations of those that commonly be called puritans, wherewithal her late parliaments have been exceedingly importuned'. None the less, as we have seen, an attempt was made by Anthony Cope, member for Banbury, to introduce measures for 'a learned ministry and the amendment of things amiss in the ecclesiastical state'. The queen sent for Cope's petition and book before they could be read, an action which prompted Peter Wentworth to another effusion asking 'whether it be not against the orders of this council to make any secret . . . which is here in hand, known to the Prince or any other'. Wentworth was removed to the Tower. Cope and three other members joined him the next day. The question of whether parliamentary liberties had been violated was raised by Sir John Heigham, one of the knights of the shire for Suffolk, and later by the diarist Thomas Cromwell; a committee was set up consisting of the privy councillors with seats in the House and nine other members, but nothing is known about its deliberations, or whether Wentworth and his colleagues were released before the end of the session. In the parliament of 1593 James Morice, an attorney of the court of wards, launched a set-piece attack on the court of high commission and on episcopal authority, implying that both were contrary to Magna Carta. For this, Neale believed that he deserved 'a place on Liberty's long and honoured roll'. The queen thought differently. She sent for the speaker and commanded 'expressly, that they should not intermeddle at all with any matter of state, or touching causes ecclesiastical'. Morice and six others were put into the custody of Sir John Fortescue, the chancellor of the exchequer. However, on this occasion the House made very little fuss about its absent members, and when told by councillors that 'the House must not call the queen to account for what she doth of her royal authority', sat in silence.

Elizabeth thus constantly claimed that matters concerning the church should not be discussed without the explicit consent of herself or her bishops. This meant, according to Job Throckmorton in a speech he wrote for the 1587 session, that the Commons were being given no more than 'a show of freedom', for they could talk freely only if 'ye meddle neither with the reformation of religion nor the establishment of succession, the very pillars and ground of all our bliss and happiness'. In this, if in nothing else, Elizabeth was an innovator. During the reigns of Henry VII and Henry VIII the iniquities of the clergy had been a topic frequently discussed in parliament. In Henry VIII's reign, and that of his elder daughter, the even more delicate question of royal marriages had also been discussed: as Yelverton put it in 1571, then 'all matters not treason or too much to the derogation of the imperial crown was tolerable there, where all things came to be considered of, and where there was such fulness of power as even the right of the crown was to be determined'. Things were very different under Elizabeth. Far from 'winning the initiative' in Elizabeth's reign, the House of Commons then faced a determined assault upon its freedom of debate, an assault which gradually beat it back.

Foreign Policy and the Succession

From the first break with Rome, matters of religion had been inextricably intertwined with questions of foreign policy. Henry, Edward, and Elizabeth were haunted by the notion of a Catholic crusade, blessed and abetted by the pope, and their pursuit of allies, as well as their treatment of Scotland and Ireland, was governed by that fear. However, although many English-men undoubtedly shared their monarch's anxiety, foreign policy was rarely discussed in parliament, for it was held to be a matter of royal prerogative. This convention, understandable in a period in which so much foreign policy turned on dynastic matters, was rarely breached in the sixteenth century, although, of course, the Commons might make their feelings about a particular war or alliance clear when asked to make a grant of taxation.

The only occasion on which parliament tried to dictate to Elizabeth about foreign-policy matters was in 1587 when some members sought to persuade her to do more to assist the rebels in the Low Countries: a committee of the Commons seems then to have toyed with the idea of offering a benevolence—that is, a free gift—provided that Elizabeth would take upon herself the sover-eignty of the Netherlands. Various members made lengthy speeches on foreign affairs, and Job Throckmorton, noting that 'the Lord hath vowed himself to the English', made some unwise criticisms of James VI which resulted in his own imprisonment a few days later. As Christopher Hatton observed, it was 'such a consultation as this Realm has not known for these hundred years'. However, someone warned the committee off, and the queen in any case refused the benevolence.

But if Elizabeth faced little criticism in parliament about her conduct of foreign policy she found herself constantly under attack on another, but related, front. This was the succession. The 1559 act recognizing Elizabeth had rested her claim to the throne upon the Henrician statute of 1543 rather than on any hereditary right: 'our declaration, confession and recognition, as also the limitation and declaration of the succession of the imperial crown of this realm . . . contained in the said act . . . shall stand, be, and remain the law of this realm for ever'. In its dependence upon an earlier statute the 1559 act was quite differ-ent from that passed at the beginning of Mary's reign, and it made possible the argument that since Elizabeth's title was a statutory one, parliament should be included in any consequent considera-tion of the matter—as Robert Monson suggested in 1571, 'it were horrible treason . . . to say that the parliament hath not authority to determine of the crown', for that would invalidate both the 1543 and 1559 acts.

There were, however, considerable practical difficulties involved in parliament's claim to any part in the determining of the succession. These can be seen in a bill drafted in 1563, which proposed that if there were to be a disputed succession after the queen's death, the privy council should continue to govern whilst parliament decided whose claim to the throne was the strongest. This scheme had Cecil's blessing, and he was later, in 1584, to draw up a similar plan whereby members of the last parliament to have sat were to be reassembled to determine the succession. But parliament at this time had no machinery by which it could assemble without a summons from the monarch, nor any standing after a monarch's death, facts which fatally reduced its ability to deal with a disputed succession. As Peter Wentworth pointed out in his own pamphlet on the subject, who 'shall call this parliament? Or at whose commandment will the States assemble? for that after her majesty's breath is out of her body, her majesty's privy council then is no more a council.'

Elizabeth's reaction in 1563 to both this proposal and petitions from Lords and Commons asking her to marry was entirely negative. In 1566, as we shall see, Paul Wentworth's tactic of intertwining the problems of the succession with the grant of the subsidy led to considerable difficulties for the government. By the time of the next parliament, in 1571, the situation had been further complicated by the flight to England of Mary, Queen of Scots, by the Northern Rising, and by various other plots. The issue of the succession was now inextricably intertwined with religious problems. Thomas Norton, perhaps encouraged by some of the council, tried to add to a government treason bill a clause which would have prevented anyone who had ever questioned the validity of Elizabeth's title from succeeding to the throne: Norton's purpose was to exclude the Catholic Mary Stuart, who had frequently asserted the superiority of her own claim to the English throne. (Norton also wanted to add a clause to the effect that 'whosoever shall say that the court of Parliament hath not authority to enact and bind the title of the crown . . . be adjudged a traitor'.) His major proposal was disliked by some members, who were anxious about the concept of retrospective legislation, and most of those involved in the discussions were also well aware of the queen's hostility to the scheme. None the less, in a close vote the bill was passed. The Lords then added a

clause permitting the queen to reinstate by proclamation anyone
excluded by the bill. Finally, a joint committee of the two Houses
drafted a new measure on the general lines of Norton's proposal,
but without any retrospective element—the provision would
apply only to offences committed after the parliament had ended.
This compromise was passed.

The whole matter came up again the next year in the fresh crisis
that arose from Mary's plotting with Thomas Howard, fourth
duke of Norfolk. A number of those sitting in the parliament of
1572 wanted to force Elizabeth to execute Norfolk, and they
pressed for sterner action against Mary herself than Elizabeth was
prepared to sanction. The House of Commons adjourned for a
few days to allow members to compile papers to be presented by
the speaker to the queen, and a committee was set up to assist him
in his task. The tone of the debates can be discerned from some of
these drafts: one claimed that Mary had 'heaped together all the
sins of the licentious sons of David: adultery, murder, conspiracy, treasons and blasphemies against God'. Even Norfolk's
execution did not still the clamour against Mary, Norton com-
menting ominously when a bill against her received its third
reading that 'the examples of the Old Testament be not few for
the putting of wicked kings to death'. Elizabeth could stem the
flood only by a dissolution.

There were further discussions of the succession in 1576 and in
1584, when the demands of the Commons for Mary's execution
became vociferous. The privy council had already taken a lead
with the bond of association, which sought to exclude from the
throne not only anyone who had procured an attempt on the
queen's life but also that individual's heirs. Elizabeth personally,
and successfully, defended James's claim in parliament. The
parliament of 1586, sitting whilst Mary's trial went on at
Fotheringay, witnessed continuing conflict, with parliament urging
Elizabeth into action she did not wish to take. However, time
was to ease this problem: Mary was executed before the second
session of the parliament.

Her subjects also came in time to accept Elizabeth's determination to remain single. When, in 1593, Peter Wentworth arranged
a meeting in Lincoln's Inn before the opening of parliament to
discuss the problem of the succession, he met with little encouragement, and his pamphlet *A Pithie Exhortation to her Majesty for*

establishing her successor to the crowne was largely ignored. The only result of Wentworth's efforts was his own imprisonment in the Tower, where, four years later, he died. His former parliament-ary colleagues do not appear to have mourned over-much.

Thus, the question of the succession caused considerable ten-sion in parliament during the first three decades of Elizabeth's reign, tension increased by parliament's claim that the matter was of such importance to everyone in the realm that it should be openly discussed. However, tension and the conflict over the prerogative that it provoked disappeared as soon as the problem itself was settled. Had the Stuart dynasty been as threatened by succession problems as the Tudors had been, things might have been very different, but on this issue cordiality reigned from the mid 1580s onwards.

Catholicism

However, if conflict over the succession did not permanently sour relations between the queen and her parliaments, it did have a very considerable effect on one group of her subjects. This was the Catholics. Most Englishmen seem to have been content to live in peace with their Catholic neighbours—indeed, they were not very anxious to discover which of their neighbours were Catholic—but this did not prevent waves of popular hysteria about foreign Catholic powers and papistry in high places sweep-ing the country from time to time. Those in parliament were by no means immune from such fears. Although few members were as rabidly anti-Catholic as the unpleasant Richard Topcliffe, debates after the Northern Rising and the publication of the papal bull excommunicating the queen reveal that many of them believed that they could provide illustrations of Thomas Scott's theory that 'papistry [is] the principal which hath produced rebellion'. In the 1580s members were likewise anxious to blacken the name of the king of Spain, and to utter dire warnings about the missionary priests coming in from Douai.

When it came to translating such wild talk into statutes, Elizabeth's parliaments were more cautious. This caution may have stemmed from the fact that despite the provisions of the 1563 supremacy oath act, which extended the range of those subject to the oath of supremacy (clerics, judges, justices, and mayors) to include all those taking holy orders, graduates, school-masters, lawyers, and members of the Commons—peers were not so required—many Catholics and Catholic sympathizers remained in the Lower House. The History of Parliament Trust has suggested that over 30 per cent of Elizabethan members were Catholic, 'church Catholics', or had an immediate member of their family who was a Catholic. Certainly it is suprisingly easy to pick out men such as Francis Stonor, who sat for Woodstock in 1586 despite having earlier allowed his house to be used for clandestine Catholic printing, Nicholas Potts, who died in 1623 'a member of the true, ancient, apostolic church', but sat for Bedford in 1584, and Oliver Manners and Toby Matthew, both of whom later became Catholic priests. Sir Herbert Croft, who sat in four Elizabethan parliaments and two Jacobean ones, was to retire to Douai in 1617 to live with the Benedictines in 'pauper celle tanquam monarchus'.

Despite such men, statutes were passed in 1571 making it treason to say that Elizabeth was a heretic or schismatic, or to bring in papal bulls. However, a bill in the same parliament enabling the queen temporarily to confiscate the property of Catholic exiles provoked 'many arguments'; although finally passed, both this bill and an explanatory measure of the following year raised the same anxieties about property rights as those that had so worried members in 1555 (see above, pp. 83–4). In 1581 an act 'to retain the queen's subjects in due obedience' made it treasonable to seek to withdraw the queen's subjects from their allegiance to her or to the Church of England. This act also made everyone over 16 who did not go to church liable to a fine of £20 per month. Three years later, in the aftermath of the assassination of William of Orange, an act 'against jesuits and seminary priests' turned everyone ordained under the authority of Rome since the first year of Elizabeth's reign into a traitor. (This, as Philip Hughes pointed out, was the statute under which 123 of the 146 people put to death between 1585 and Elizabeth's death were indicted.[10]) By 1593, however, there was little support in parliament for vindictive anti-Catholic legislation: the threat of a Catholic heir had disappeared, and the Armada's defeat had given the lie to the notion of Spanish invincibility.

It is an indication of the continuing feebleness of convocation as a legislative body that this whole matter was left to parliament.

Although in the meeting of 1563 severe measures against Catholics were proposed, they were largely unsuccessful, and the division that was then apparent between the radicals in the Lower House and the more politically prudent bishops emasculated convocation further. Of course, the question of the Catholics was closely linked to that of the succession, and the succession had fallen within the remit of parliament since Henry VIII's marital problems of the 1530s, but the more general invasion of parliament into territory once held by convocation was undoubtedly strengthened by these statutes. In 1559 convocation had protested that authority in matters of faith and discipline belonged to the clergy 'et non ad laicos'; the events of Elizabeth's reign reinforced Richard Hooker's assertion of 1593 that it is 'a thing most consonant with equity and reason that no ecclesiastical laws be made in a Christian commonwealth without consent of the laity as of the clergy'.

Anti-Catholic feeling was closely related to what was going on—or was thought to be going on—abroad, and was also, like Puritan enthusiasm, indissolubly linked with the problem of the succession. As time solved that problem, Puritan zeal and hostility towards Catholics also diminished. The radicals in the Commons died, or, like Strickland and Cope, fell silent. (Although he sat in four more parliaments in Elizabeth's reign, Cope is never known to have spoken in the Commons after his imprisonment in 1587; he tried once, after an interval of ten years, but failed to catch the speaker's eye.) By 1593, as we have noted, anxiety in the Commons about Protestant sectaries had grown, whilst fear of Catholics had diminished. Thus, although hostility to international Catholicism caused Elizabeth difficulties in her handling of the Commons, that enthusiasm was dimmed in her later parliaments, and the difficulties consequently reduced.

Economic and Social Matters

Much parliamentary time was taken up, however, not with major political questions such as the state of the church or the establishment of the succession, but with affairs of the commonwealth, that is, social and economic matters. Bills were introduced into Elizabethan parliaments dealing with an astonishing range of topics from education to law reform, from a proposal to protect the realm by insisting that imported hops should be free of 'dross, sand or leaves' to an attempt to compel people to wear caps and not hats on holidays. Over one-quarter of the bills introduced in Elizabeth's later parliaments touched economic and social matters, and nearly another quarter dealt with local affairs—sessions in Caernarfon, orphans in Monmouth, and coals in Newcastle. Such proposals were frequently unsuccessful, but might reappear in the next session, and the next, and the next. Some topics seem to have been hardy perennials of the parliamentary garden— proposals for a uniform system of weights and measures was one such.

Unsuccessful bills, of which the only record is a laconic statement in one of the Journals, make quantitative statements about Tudor parliaments and their efficiency extremely difficult. Even where bills were successful, the historian may find tracing their origins and progress problematic. It is rarely possible to make definite statements about the role of the government and that of private initiative in prompting social and economic legislation. In general, it is probably safest to assume that most proposals stemmed from the concern of private individuals and groups unless there is clear evidence of government intervention. The government did sometimes play an important role in formulating such measures—Sir Geoffrey Elton has shown, for example, how the council drafted the regulations relating to apprenticeship and wages, which became, after the House of Commons had considerably modified the bill and inserted various exemptions, the 1563 statute of artificers.[11] Sometimes the government even took over a private initiative bill that had failed: in 1572, for instance, the council, faced with the problem of replacing the expiring poor law of 1563, revived a measure that had been unsuccessful in the previous year.

However, government initiative was rarely necessary in social matters, for individual members of both Houses clearly felt very great concern about the problems of their age: thirteen bills dealing with drunkenness and inns were discussed between 1576 and 1601, for example.[12] Strong arguments were produced in favour of the regulation of personal conduct—drunkenness, for instance, was considered by some as a reason for the scarcity and high price of grain. However, this concern, although vocal, had less positive impact than might have been expected. Although many members saw drunkeness as a threat to social and moral order, bills to regulate inns were unsuccessful in 1576, 1581, 1584, 1589, 1593, and in 1601, when six different bills were discussed. Failures resulted in part from anxiety lest the justices of the peace when enforcing such legislation should not confine themselves to the 'meaner sort', but also attack the upper classes: Henry Unton declared in the 1593 debates on bastardy that it would be appalling if 'gentlemen or men of quality' should be 'put to such a shame' as to be whipped. In the 1601 debate on a bill designed to deter people from going to an inn within two miles of their home, one member argued that

it was a common and usual thing in Lancashire and those parts for gentlemen as they go a-hawking to go and take a repast at an ale-house: yea, men sometimes of 500 marks a year: but, Mr Speaker, I hope these men are not intended to come within this bill. And for the act itself, I think it a mere cobweb to catch flies in.

Members were also not entirely convinced that legislation was a suitable way of dealing with such problems. Not all would have gone as far as John Bond, who argued in 1601 that 'every evil in a state is not to be met with in a law. And as it is in the natural, so it is in the politique body, that sometimes the remedy is worse than the disease. And therefore particular laws against particular offences produce novelty, and in novelty, contempt', but many resented the interference of crown and council in matters of personal conduct. Others perhaps felt, as Edward Glascock did in 1601, that some topics were 'fitter to be spoken of in a pulpit than a parliament'.

Members of the Commons were none the less sensitive to changing social and economic circumstances. In 1597, a time of high prices and disease, at least eleven draft bills dealing with poor relief and vagabondage, the erection of hospitals, and the setting-up of houses of correction were introduced into the Commons. Out of these finally emerged three measures. One, against vagabondage, ran into difficulties in the Lords, who substituted a bill of their own. The Commons rejected this by 106 votes to 66, but a compromise measure was finally passed. A second measure, for the relief of the poor, provided, together with the 1601 act, the basis for the poor law of the next 250 years. The third act was for hospitals.

It was also decided in 1597 to revive the anti-enclosure legislation repealed four years earlier. A great deal of social concern was expressed in the course of these debates: 'the eyes of the poor', said one speaker, 'are upon this parliament, and sad for the want they suffer'. However, some members were made of sterner stuff. Henry Jackman refused to believe that high prices were the result of pasture farming, blaming instead the weather. Attuned, as a cloth merchant, to the needs of the clothiers, Jackman argued that a restoration of tillage would push up the cost of cloth, which would lead to more beggars. And if the return to tillage produced a glut of corn, prices would slump and farmers would be unable to pay their rents. 'Men are not to be compelled by penalties, but allured by profit, to any good exercise', he said.

Certainly a major problem in securing such general legislation was, as we have seen, the need to balance the interests of different groups—in this instance, graziers and clothiers. One way of doing this was by permitting exceptions to a general statute—for instance, in the 1597 anti-enclosure statute which acknowledged that what was beneficial in some areas would be prejudicial to others. Various members secured exclusion clauses for their own regions—Thomas Harris, burgess for Bossiney, managed to exclude Cornwall from the working of the bill, and the Shropshire men secured a proviso exempting their county, which was said to be fittest to be grass and dairy. Problems remained, however, and when prices fell in 1601 the question of repealing the 1597 statute was raised. One member noted that 'in the time of dearth, when we made this statute, it was not considered that the hand of God was upon us, and now corn is cheap'. He went on to point out the problem of reconciling the needs of the buyer with those of the grower: if corn is too cheap, he said, 'the husbandman is undone' and 'we must provide for [him] for he is the staple man of the kingdom'. Robert Cecil and other members of the government were not in favour of repeal, however, and the act stayed.

It is, on the face of it, surprising that the Commons continued to show an interest in industrial and commercial matters, for members of the Lower House were drawn more and more from the gentry: by the end of the sixteenth century no more than 15 per cent of borough seats were filled by merchants or tradesmen. But, paradoxically, at the same time as the House became dominated by gentlemen, gentlemen had become more involved in trade.

The development of the joint-stock company, which made it possible for non-active members to invest in trading ventures, was crucial here: thus, for example, the Russia Company at its foundation in 1555 included amongst its members seven peers, eight office-holders, fourteen knights, seventeen aldermen, eleven esquires, and eleven gentlemen. (It is interesting to find that the Company secured a private act safeguarding its trading monopoly in the parliament of 1566.) By 1621 the involvement of a number of members in the affairs of the Virginia Company was substantial enough to have a very considerable impact on events in parliament, but members had long before that been upholding or attacking trading companies as they affected themselves.

Moreover, interested groups had become very skilled at manipulating members to their own advantage. The great London companies, and in particular the Clothworkers', were adept at lobbying.[13] They enlisted the assistance of the speaker and of privy councillors, they gave dinners and presents to sympathetic members, and they tried to ensure that their bills were read only when their friends were present in the Chamber. In 1581, another London company, the Armourers', obtained a list of members from the crown office from which to identify those who might be sympathetic towards an Armourers' bill. Nine dinners were given by the Company for members of the Lower House, and gloves, capons, and cash were bestowed on selected individuals.[14] The Armourers also prepared papers setting out the arguments in favour of their bill, as the Curriers had done in 1571 and the Brewers were to do in 1593. On more than one occasion the Curriers, a politically experienced company, spent half their annual income on their suit—in fees, copies of the list of members of both Houses, and *douceurs*.[15]

One result of such activity was to clog up the parliamentary process with numerous bills for 'occupation, misteries and companies'. Although bills of this sort may have been of high importance to the individuals involved, government business always had priority, and they were often frustrated. None the less, the fact that companies and trades looked to parliament and its members as a means whereby their interests might be advanced resulted in the development of sophisticated political techniques: commerce, not Protestantism, taught the House of Commons the importance of management skills.

Taxation

Elizabeth was the first of the Tudors to ask for taxation in the first parliamentary session of a reign, and she went on to demand a grant in each of her subsequent parliaments save that of 1572. One reason for the frequency of her tax demands was the diminishing sum raised by each separate grant. The yield of the fifteenth and tenth, fixed in 1334, was seriously out of date, and in Elizabeth's reign the sum produced by the newer subsidy also fell from its earlier peak of £140,000 to about £85,000. The only part of the subsidy from which the yield improved at this time was that raised from the clergy, which by the 1590s was producing the comparatively large annual sum of £10,000–£12,000.

The subsidy suffered from the ability of the most powerful to persuade the county commissioners to portray them as poorer than they were. Thus, as Latimer said in a sermon during Edward's reign, 'his cattle, corn, sheep, in every man's eyes, shall be worth £200, besides other things, as money and plate; he will marry [off] his daughter, and give her 400 or 500 marks, and yet at the valuation he will be a £20 man'. The nobility, who assessed themselves, constantly presented their position as worse than it was: Burghley himself, at the end of his life, when his income was about £4,000 p.a., was assessed at £133. 6s. 8d. This tendency to under-assessment, which appears to have grown worse in Elizabeth's reign, was exacerbated by the fact that other levies, such as that for the upkeep of the militia, were based on the same assessment: as one member noted in 1593,

I should well agree to the subsidies if they might not be prejudicial to the subject in other services . . . according to a man's valuation in subsidy are they at all other charges as to the wars and in time of muster with horse and armour; and this charge maketh men unwilling to be raised in the subsidy.

Elizabeth sought to overcome these problems by the simple expedient of multiple grants: fifteenths and tenths were granted in pairs, then in the 1590s in sixes, and finally, in 1601, eight were granted, whilst there was a grant of two subsidies in 1589, three in 1593, and four in 1601. She was unwilling to experiment with new forms of taxation: indeed, her vice-chamberlain, Sir Thomas Heneage, declared in 1593 that she was positively opposed to change. Faced by a suggestion from Sir Henry Knyvet that a yearly levy should be provided, based on a new survey of all men's lands and goods, Heneage urged the House of Commons to follow 'the wonted course'. He said that he had heard the queen say 'that she loved not such fineness of device and novel inventions, but liked rather to have the ancient usages offered'.

This conservatism had not existed earlier in the century. Under Henry VII and his son various forms of poll-tax had been tried before the subsidy finally emerged in an acceptable form. Edward VI's government in 1549 had tried a radical new policy with a measure that taxed home-produced cloth and sheep (see above, p. 88). Thereafter, there was no experimentation with taxation. The consequences of this conservative approach were to be very serious for the Stuarts.

By the end of her reign Elizabeth was, moreover, heavily dependent on parliamentary supply. Initially, however, she had benefited from the reform of the customs undertaken by her sister: in 1558 Mary had introduced a new book of 'rates', that is, the theoretical valuations of goods on which customs duties were charged. The 1558 book added an additional customs burden of 75 per cent, and revenue rose from £29,000 in 1556/7 to £83,000 in 1558/9. Interestingly, this substantial increase produced a number of complaints to the privy council, but no opposition in parliament. Minor revisions of the Book of Rates took place in 1583 and 1590, but there was no substantial revision of the book until 1608: that revision, which raised prices 30–40 per cent, provoked lengthy parliamentary debate in 1610. Mary was then much criticized, and blamed for another pernicious habit, that of levying extra duties, or 'impositions', on particular goods. One member, Fuller, claimed that Mary, 'marrying with a stranger, began a strange and new course of imposition . . . being seduced by foreign advice'. Why this had been allowed to happen without parliamentary comment, and why things changed so much under the Stuarts, is something yet to be explained by those who wish to eliminate conflict from the reign of James I.

Because she neither experimented with new forms of taxation nor kept her customs assessments up to date, and because the income from crown lands was diminishing under the impact of sales, Elizabeth required a great number of parliamentary grants.

Perhaps surprisingly, she rarely encountered any opposition to her demands for taxation, frequent though they were. Indeed, the crown's decisions about the purpose for which the grant of taxation was being sought had been accepted throughout the sixteenth century, even the size of the grant being, as we have seen, only rarely a subject of controversy. In 1563 the subsidy bill was held up because of opposition to a provision that taxpayers should swear to the truth of their assessments, although everyone openly acknowledged these were wildly inaccurate. The demand was dropped. Three years later, in the second session of the same parliament, Elizabeth again, as we shall see, encountered problems over the subsidy bill. Thereafter, her requests for aid were met without difficulty, although in 1589 Henry Jackman, burgess for Calne, did oppose the levying of a second subsidy. Jackman argued that the second subsidy was unnecessary since England's greatest enemy, Spain, had been defeated the previous year, and that in any case, since it was not to be paid for three years, it would be too late for defence. His colleagues in parliament could easily find the money, Jackman said, but the tax would produce 'suits, exclamations, complaints and lamentations' from the poor, besides being a dangerous precedent. However, Jackman's words do not appear to have aroused much response amongst his colleagues. Thereafter Elizabeth's requests were met with alacrity, despite the heavy burdens being placed on local communities in other ways.

For most of the first half of Elizabeth's reign she was at peace, which makes the ease with which she secured grants of taxation the more remarkable. Neale, indeed, said of her request for a subsidy in 1566: 'however justified nationally and morally, Elizabeth was here on dangerous ground. She would be asking for taxes in time of peace, for extraordinary revenues in ordinary circumstances . . . it was a sorry outlook'.[16] However, it should be noted that although early seventeenth-century opponents of the crown were certainly to argue that the king should normally 'live of his own', and that he could ask for additional income only in a national emergency, this was a notion that originated in the political and legal circumstances of the time: as we have seen, in the 1530s, 1540s, and 1550s monarchs had frequently secured grants of taxation in peacetime, and Elizabeth was merely following in their footsteps.

None the less, the House of Commons clearly preferred to justify its grants by reference to military need. Thus, after the subsidy act of 1559, which was justified primarily in terms of the bad state of royal finances, military and defensive needs were always mentioned in the preamble to Elizabethan subsidy acts, as well as the notion that some return was due to the queen for her good government. Moreover, when requesting a grant of taxation the crown itself usually drew attention to the military situation: in 1566, for instance, Sir Ralph Sadler declared that 'it is a point of wisdom in the time of peace to provide for the war', and in 1571 the lord keeper's speech began by mentioning the cost of suppressing the rebellion in the North and went on to explain that the queen's debts had also grown because of a decline in customs dues. In 1576 Mildmay told the Commons that 'as wise mariners do then most diligently prepare their tackle and provide to withstand a tempest that may happen, so in this our blessed time of peace . . . we ought . . . to make provision'. Defensive and military needs were always mentioned somewhere in subsidy preambles, a fact which must lead to some qualification of the notion that an entirely new principle of taxation was introduced in the sixteenth century.

There is little doubt that those making grants had the ordinary requirements of peacetime government at the back of their minds as they did so: indeed, the ordinary expenditure of the crown was now so great that only extraordinary grants could cover it.[17] Perhaps as little as two-thirds of the taxation granted under Edward had been used for war and defence; the remainder went towards the ordinary—that is, the routine—expenses of government. Five to ten per cent of the grant made under the war conditions of 1558 was used for the ordinary expenditure of government, and taxation was thereafter an important component of regular royal finance. The attempt in the Great Contract of 1610 to exchange the prerogative rights of wardship and purveyance for a regular annual income was therefore no more than a recognition of an existing state of affairs. However, this fact was never openly acknowledged: monarch and parliament alike shrouded their requests for and their grants of taxation in the customary language of defensive necessity, irrespective of the real needs of the time.

Whatever the justification for the grant, the monarch liked to

be asking from a position of strength. If members believed that
the country was being asked to grant taxation only to pay for the
frivolities of courtiers they were naturally reluctant to consent.
Elizabeth's ministers, in particular, constantly stressed the
frugality of her personal expenditure compared with that of her
predecessors—in 1571, for example, Mildmay declared that the
queen 'lived in most temperate manner, without excess, either in
building or other superfluous things of pleasure', and in 1593 the
chancellor declared that 'in buildings she hath consumed little or
nothing, in her pleasure not much. As for her apparel, it is royal
and prince-like, beseeming her calling, but not superfluous nor
excessive. The charges of her house small, yea, never less in any
king's time.' Francis Bacon, anxious to win back royal favour in
the next parliament, pointed out that the queen did not spend
upon

excessive and exorbitant donatives, nor upon sumptuous and unnecessary triumphs, buildings or like magnificence, but upon the preservation,
protection and honour of the realm . . . Sure I am that the treasure that
cometh from you to her majesty is but a vapour which riseth from the
earth and gathereth into a cloud and there stayeth not long, but upon the
same earth it falleth again.

In justifying its requests with a demonstration of good house-
keeping the crown had sound medieval precedents. However, a
distinction was drawn between an assertion of good management
and a blow-by-blow account of how the money had been spent,
which was not considered a suitable matter for parliamentary
debate. Thus, when warned by Cecil in 1553 that parliament
might ask why so much royal land and revenues had been given
away, the duke of Northumberland declared firmly:

we need not be so ceremonious as to imagine the objections of every
forward person, but rather to burden their minds and hearts with the
king's debts and necessities, grown and risen by such occasions and
means as can be denied to no man . . . we need not to seem to make
account to the Commons of his majesty's liberality and bountifulness in
augmenting or advancing of his nobles, or of his benevolences shown to
any of his good servants.

Similarly, in 1576 Mildmay told the House of Commons that
'her majesty is not to yield an account how she spendeth her

treasure', although he then added, 'yet for your satisfaction I will let you understand such things as are very true'.

The assumption, then, was that the crown should not seek taxation for frivolous purposes, or because it had misspent its revenues. On the other hand, it was also assumed that the country should contribute to the extraordinary needs of government, however these were defined.

The role of the Commons, as representatives of the shires and boroughs which had sent them, was much more important in the granting of taxation than that of the Lords (see above, p. 51). The Lords rarely amended money bills, and in 1584 the queen even asked that the Lords should adjourn for two days whilst the Commons considered the subsidy bill. In 1593, however, there was a dispute between the two Houses over a money bill. After the Commons had nominated a committee to consider the subsidy, the Lords asked for a joint conference. At this, Burghley declared that the two subsidies being offered were insufficient for the crown's needs, and he suggested that the Commons should think again. When this was reported back, Francis Bacon declared that although he thought Burghley was correct and that three subsidies should be granted, he was hostile in principle to interventions from the Upper House in such matters. Much discussion followed, and after Robert Beale had found a precedent from the reign of Henry IV it was decided that the Commons would refuse further conferences with the Lords over the subsidy. Sir Henry Unton, knight for Buckinghamshire, told the House that 'in matters of subsidy and contribution we might not be governed or directed' by the Lords, for 'we are far more interested therein than they. They offer but a small portion for themselves, we both for ourselves and infinite thousands besides . . . we are stewards of many more purses than they'. He concluded by demanding, 'let the first resolution be ours, the thanks ours and the honour ours'. Eventually, after a great deal of soothing by privy councillors and courtiers, the House calmed down and the subsidy bill was passed.

A major constitutional clash over the Commons' right to initiate money bills had been avoided. Unton, none the less, was thereafter in deep disgrace with the queen: the earl of Essex told him that 'she startles at your name, chargeth you with popularity and hath every particular of your speeches in parliament without book'. The Commons remained sensitive too: John Hare, member for Horsham, told Robert Cecil in the next parliament that he was unwilling 'to assent unto any certain payment until their lordships were first conferred with', since in 1593, when the Lords had intervened to raise the grant, 'we lost part of our thanks'. However, although the clash raised profound constitutional questions, there is no reason to believe that Burghley ever intended to dispute the Commons' right to initiate money bills: now an old man, he was merely less attuned than he had once been to the delicate sensitivities of the Lower House.

In England at this time, unlike, for instance, the kingdom of Aragon, there existed no real tradition that supply was dependent on the redress of grievances, and there is only one clear example in the sixteenth century of the idea being floated. This was in 1566. The parliamentary meeting of 1566 was one in which considerable friction arose over Elizabeth's reluctance to commit herself to marrying and settling the succession. As a result the subsidy bill was held up: the Venetian ambassador reported that the Commons had said that they would first discuss the succession and then afterwards debate those matters that the queen wanted. Elizabeth then sent a message ordering the House to content itself with her promise of marriage, which prompted Paul Wentworth to ask if the queen's message were not 'against the liberties of the House', whereupon 'arose divers arguments, continuing from nine of the clock until two after noon'.

Elizabeth was forced to compromise: in a carefully worded message she declared that she had not intended 'to prejudice any part of the laudable liberties heretofore granted to them freely communing without commandment or constraint'. She also abandoned one-third of the proposed subsidy. Even then, things did not go as she wished. Those who drafted the preamble to the subsidy bill—and they included William Cecil—put into it a passage thanking the queen for her promise to marry and settle the succession. Elizabeth was furious when shown a draft of this preamble, and wrote on it:

I know no reason why any my private answers to the realm should serve for prologue to a subsidies book. Neither yet do I understand why such audacity should be used to make without my licence an act of my words

. . . Is there no hold of my speech without an act compel me to confirm?
Shall my princely consent be turned to strengthen my words that be not
of themselves substantives?

The preamble was toned down.[18]

This was, in fact, one of Elizabeth's most difficult parliaments,
largely because her refusal to commit herself over the succession
was much disliked not only by those in parliament but also by
many of her privy council. It was an apparently dangerous
precedent.

However, it was not, in the event, a precedent upon which the
Commons chose to build, and the relationship between supply
and the redress of grievances remained a subtle one. For instance,
in the course of the 1571 debates Robert Bell declared that
although 'a subsidy was by every good subject to be yielded
unto', it would in practice be difficult to collect because of the
burden of 'licences and the abuse of promoters . . . If a burden
should be laid on the back of the Commons, and no redress of the
common evils', he said, 'then there might haply ensue, that they
would lay down the burden in the midst of the way, and turn to
the contrary of their duties'. John Popham went on to speak of
crown officials who used royal money for their own purposes,
and William Lovelace about purveyors and fines levied for respite
of homage. The House agreed to set up a committee to draft bills
dealing with some of these problems: a bill 'against promoters'
was passed by both Houses, although it eventually lapsed. The
queen was forced into activity, sending a message to say that she
would 'take order for licences, wherein she hath been careful, and
more careful would be'.

Here is a complicated counterpoint of grievance, supply, and
redress. Members were very realistic about how the whole thing
operated: in 1584 one remarked, 'her majesty, expecting a benevolence, from [us], will the sooner yield to [our] lawful and
necessary petitions'. Occasionally members may have dragged
their feet over the subsidy bill simply because they feared that
passing it might bring an end to the session: in 1589, for instance,
there was some anxiety lest the parliament would be ended if the
subsidy bill were passed very quickly, but in fact the parliament
went on for another month. In 1601, during the tense debates on
monopolies, Robert Wingfield explicitly requested, 'seeing the

subsidy was granted, and they had yet done nothing', that 'it would please her Majesty not to dissolve the parliament until some acts were passed'. Despite these fears, parliaments always did remain sitting some time after the subsidy bill had been passed.

Thus, the Tudors had managed to prevent the principle of no supply without redress of grievance becoming a rule. However —and it is an important point—they did not succeed in creating a system whereby grants were made before any discussion of grievances. Members knew that a subtle relationship existed between their willingness to grant the subsidy and the monarch's willingness to redress grievances, and they occasionally exploited that knowledge. But the monarch had her own strength in the fact that it was she alone who decided when parliament should end, something of which she frequently reminded the Commons. Both sides coupled the granting of taxation with the redressing of grievances, but they did so in a manner that provided a commentary on the constitution, rather than being a part of it.

Prerogative Finance

Under Elizabeth, as under the earlier Tudors, requests for taxation were generally accepted without difficulty. Few other aspects of royal finance were ever discussed in parliament— forced loans, for example, were mentioned only when the monarch sought to be relieved of his obligation to repay them (see above, pp. 15–16). However, the crown was still in the sixteenth century heavily dependent upon its income from land and feudal rights, and certain of these feudal and prerogative rights produced occasional skirmishes in parliament: these were wardship, purveyance, and respite of homage.

A feudal lord had the right to look after the lands and the person of a minor heir until he was 21, if male, or 14, if female. There was no accountability for his stewardship, and lords unashamedly helped themselves to the profits of the land during a minority: as Thomas Smith declared, 'he who had a father which kept a good house . . . shall come to his own after he is out of wardship, woods decayed, houses fallen down, stock wasted and gone, lands let forth and ploughed to the barren'. The lord also had the right to arrange the heir's marriage, and wards were often sold in marriage to the highest bidder, irrespective of suitability.

The monarch had priority in wardship over all other lords of whom lands had been held, and the Tudors were able to make a substantial profit from wardship. The exploitation of wardship was systematized in 1540 when Henry VIII set up the court of wards to discover and administer wardships. In Elizabeth's reign the court brought in about £15,000 p.a., but this was no more than one-quarter of the total profits of crown wardship, the remainder going to royal servants.

Although there was a constant trickle of criticism of wardship from reformers such as Latimer, comparatively little discussion was heard in parliament. However, in 1585 the crown unwittingly provoked trouble when Burghley, master of the court of wards, introduced two bills to check devices by which the crown was being defrauded. When one of these bills came from the Lords on 18 March 1585 it ran into considerable difficulties. A committee was set up, a conference of the two Houses was held, and a new bill was drafted. This bill was lost in a division on 26 March by 95 votes to 75. The bill, which made liable to wardship land which had been held of the crown by knight service and leased for more than one hundred years, was retrospective in its working, which was one reason why it was criticized—the solicitor-general was even forced into the unwise observation that 'I see no reason why a statute might not look back if there be reason why it should'. The Lords went on to pass a new bill of their own, but it received only one reading in the Commons. The force of the attack in the Commons undoubtedly stemmed from self-interest: as the solicitor-general remarked, 'it concerns you all that have manors holden of you to be thus defeated of them'. However, all those present accepted that wardship was a legitimate source of royal revenue: even William Fleetwood, who was critical of the bill, argued: 'let us give her majesty her due revenue, or else she must have subsidies and fifteenths'.

Wardship was raised in parliament again in 1598, on Burghley's death. There was then some suggestion that the revenues of wardship should be abolished in return for a fixed annual income, but the idea was not explored in detail, and in 1599 Robert Cecil succeeded his father as master of the court. Under his mastership the income rose considerably—sales of wardships, which averaged 64 per annum in the 1560s, had risen to an average of 123 by the period 1610–13—and this rise may be one reason why a proposal to abolish wardship in return for a fixed annual income was one of the first matters discussed in the parliament of 1604, and became a central issue in 1610.

Another feudal right which frequently provoked complaints in parliament was purveyance. Purveyance allowed the monarch to purchase compulsorily supplies for the royal household. It caused a whole range of difficulties and complaints: what was the prevailing price for any particular commodity? when and how would payment be made? did the right apply to the supplying of the king's own household alone, or did it include his armies? These problems had produced complaints throughout the Middle Ages. Grievances expressed in 1300, for instance, produced the articuli super cartas, which declared that prises should be taken in the future only by authorized purveyors and for the use of the king's personal household. There was further trouble in the Lincoln parliament of 1301, and in 1309 Edward II had to confirm the articuli. None the less, it was necessary in 1340 to pass a statute dealing with purveyance. And so on. Despite the fact that during the reign of Henry VIII the crown was buying at more or less the prevailing market rate, resentment continued and was exacerbated by heavy government spending in the wars of the 1540s. The author of a pamphlet entitled 'The causes of dearth' probably expressed a commonly held belief when he wrote in 1548 that purveyance increased prices and ought therefore to be abolished. A purveyor paid for a lamb worth 2s. only 12d., he declared, and for a capon worth 12d., only 6d. Moreover, the seller had to wait for his money. The author's answer to such problems was a tax to replace purveyance, based on 1d. per thousand sheep in the common fields, 2d. per thousand sheep in pastures, and so on; this tax would, he thought, bring in £17,187.

Reflecting these views, a bill was introduced in March 1549. This prohibited forcible provisioning for three years and instituted stern penalties: purveyors were to give three times the value of the goods taken if they offended against the act. In 1555 another statute was passed which made important improvements: justices of the peace were to be given a copy of the purveyor's commission, and that commission was to be in English.

None the less, trouble continued. In 1563 bills were introduced to deal with various aspects of purveyance: one was lost after passing the Commons, another, passed by both Houses, was vetoed by the queen. Robert Bell raised the subject again, as we have seen, in the course of the 1571 subsidy debate. Bell's move was seconded by a lawyer, William Lovelace, who proposed replacing purveyance with a county rate. The House ordered that a general bill should be drawn up, whilst the comptroller of the queen's household, Sir James Croft, under whose surveillance purveyance came, said that he 'would do his endeavour for reformation of all things raised by purveyors'. This largely satisfied the House. However, Sir Humphrey Gilbert unwisely declared that Bell's attempt had been 'a vain device', and a perilous one, which 'tended to the derogation of the prerogative imperial'; this speech provoked an attack by Peter Wentworth in which he described Gilbert as 'a flatterer, a liar and a naughty man', who could 'change himself to all fashions but honesty'. The only concrete result of Bell's initiative was a statute dealing with abuses that had arisen from the 1555 act for purveyors in Oxford and Cambridge.

Cecil tried to overcome the problems associated with purveyance by organizing compositions on a county basis for various commodities, whereby the counties agreed to supply the royal household annually with a fixed quantity of foodstuffs at an agreed price. None the less, trouble persisted and in 1586 both Houses passed a bill enforcing various provisions of the 1555 statute. The queen vetoed it.

The Armada campaign involved, of course, extensive use of purveyance. Complaints were voiced and in 1589 the House of Commons, led by John Hare, a London lawyer and member for Horsham, George More of Loseley, and Robert Wroth, secured the passage of a new bill. To quash this the queen acted through the House of Lords, sending a message to say that if any of her officials were misbehaving, she was herself 'both able and willing to see due reformation'. When they were told of this the Commons set up a committee to consider what they should do next. The committee recommended that the House seek an audience with the queen, and explain to her what the nature of their grievances was. At this audience the queen told the

Commons that she had already 'by the advice of her judges and learned council' set reforms in motion that would be 'as good and better for the ease of the subjects than that which the House had attempted without her privity'.

Things were undoubtedly becoming very tense. The queen took the line that purveyance was a prerogative matter, about which the Commons might petition her, but not legislate, whilst the Commons were arguing that any grievance could be remedied by a parliamentary bill. The Commons had historically much the better case, since, as we have seen, problems arising from purveyance had frequently been dealt with by statutes, including that of 1555. However, after the audience tempers cooled, and Elizabeth sent a message to the Commons suggesting that some of them should join the privy councillors and household officials in their discussions about how purveyance could be improved. Four members, including Wroth, were chosen, and it was agreed that they should receive information from other interested parties to lay before the committee.

Thereafter, purveyance ceased to be a source of dispute in Elizabethan parliaments. Throughout the 1590s composition continued—forcibly in 1592 and 1593—and it was not until the accession of James that parliament considered the matter again. In 1604 Wroth, one of the promoters of the 1589 bill, laid before the Commons a seven-point reform programme, which again included purveyance. A petition was drawn up, offering a composition in return for the abolition of pureveyance, but in the end it came to nothing.

Sometimes the irritation produced by the crown's exploitation of its feudal rights seems disproportionate to the financial benefit it thereby acquired. The crown's exploitation of the feudal duty of homage is an example of this. Many tenants-in-chief put off the need to appear in person to swear homage to their monarch by paying an annual sum to the lord chamberlain. This 'respite of homage' was disliked, or, at least, the fee it involved was resented, and in 1563 a bill to abolish respite was twice read in the Lower House but lost. In 1571 the matter came up again, and this time both Houses were involved. The Lords drafted a bill, and a conference of both Houses was held. A confrontation with the crown over the prerogative appeared inevitable, but Elizabeth saved the situation by promising to see herself that fees were reduced. There the matter rested until the Commons brought it up again in 1604.

Thus, wardship, purveyance, and respite of homage produced acrimonious debates in parliament, and raised serious questions about the queen's interpretation of her prerogative. However, none of these issues permanently soured relations between the monarch and her parliaments. But there was one other aspect of prerogative finance which was to cause a deep, and perhaps unbridgeable, rift. This was the issue of monopolies.

Monopolies were privileges granted by the monarch in letters patent to an individual or group. They fell at this period into three broad categories. The first allowed the grantee the sole right to enjoy some new invention or trade: such grants were similar to the monopolies issued today under the supervision of the patent office.

A second type of monopoly permitted an individual or group to do something despite the existence of statutes forbidding it: the monarch thus used his or her power to 'dispense' with statute and to allow something to be done, statutes to the contrary 'non obstante'. Export licences are a good example of this type of grant: sweeping restrictions had been made by statute to prevent the export of commodities such as corn, but the monarch was able by his discretionary power to vary the operations of the statute according to local and national circumstances.

The third group of monopolistic grants related to penal statutes. To deal with negligence or delinquency on the part of officials, governments in the fifteenth century had turned to penal statutes, that is, to statutes which prohibited a stated offence on pain of a pecuniary penalty. Enforcement of these statutes was encouraged by a division of the sums thus raised between the crown and the person who laid the information leading to a conviction, who was known as the promoter or informer. The number of such statutes passed in the late fifteenth and early sixteenth centuries—over a hundred in the reign of Henry VIII alone—suggests that they were generally believed to be efficacious, and their use was therefore extended to cover the regulation of trade and industry.

It was recognized, however, that many informers were greedy and unscrupulous, and efforts to regulate their behaviour were common: in 1566, for instance, Cecil suggested that some bill should be proposed in parliament to amend 'the oppression of the informers', and in 1571, when a bill was being discussed about church attendance, Fleetwood, expressing a hope that no profit should come thereby to promoters, 'showed the evils and inconveniences which did grow by these men's doings, whereby no reformation was sought but private gain to the worst sort of men'. A bill regulating informers was subsequently passed by both Houses, although the queen then vetoed it. However, another bill was more successful in the next parliament. The government also recognized a tendency for informers and offenders to act in collusion, and it therefore granted licences authorizing the recipients to issue pardons in return for cash—in effect permitting patentees to bargain with offenders against penal statutes for the right to break the law.

Elizabeth was drawn to grants of monopoly partly in an attempt to revitalize the existing system of law enforcement, and partly as a means of rewarding her servants at very little cost to herself. In 1566, for instance, William King, a yeoman of the chamber, was licensed 'to put into execution the statute . . . for the maintenance of artillery and debarring of unlawful games' in Essex, Hertfordshire, Kent, Sussex, Suffolk, and Lincolnshire, and Humphrey Gilbert was in 1571 granted the right during a seven-year period to compound with offenders against the Marian statute 'for having horse, armour and weapons'. Edward Darcy, a groom of the privy chamber, was given a licence for the searching and sealing of leather, as well as one for the sale of playing-cards.

Although there was a brief flurry of concern about licences in the parliament of 1559 nothing more seems to have been said in parliament until Robert Bell's declaration in 1571 that 'by licences a few only were enhanced, and the multitude impoverished'. In a debate the next year on the leather trade, Ralph Sekerston complained about export licences, and noted that 'my lord admiral hath one of them', and in 1576 a bill 'for the better order of such as have licence of the queen's majesty to transport anything beyond the seas' was discussed. During the 1570s a large number of grants was made, and opposition from those who suffered as a result began to grow. In his study of Elizabethan Norfolk, for example, Mr Hassell Smith has shown that by the mid 1580s magistrates, who had initially been concerned primarily 'with exposing the corrupt practices of patentees and licensees, and had not overtly opposed the grants which enabled these malpractices', began to oppose the grants themselves.[19] In 1589 the members for Norfolk and Yorkshire brought up the question of the salt monopoly, which was held by the clerk to the privy council, Sir Thomas Wilkes, who was also the burgess for Southampton. Hostility to monopolies was mounting, and in 1597 criticism poured out in parliament.

Everyone was apparently agreed upon the nature of the evil, but the problem of procedure was immense. Since the grants had been made by the queen under letters patent, the only constitutional remedy open to the Commons was a petition: as Bacon declared later, 'the use hath ever been by petition to humble ourselves unto her majesty and by petition to have our grievances remedied'. Some brave souls none the less suggested in 1597 that a bill should be drafted, but Elizabeth, with sound tactical sense, had meanwhile ordered that all patents should be examined. A few patents were subsequently abolished, but not enough to appease the discontented, and a full-scale attack was therefore launched in the parliament of 1601.

The tone of the debate can be gathered from the speeches on 20 November. Mr Martin, for instance, declared that

the principal commodities both of my town and country are engrossed into the hands of those blood-suckers of the common wealth . . . If these blood-suckers still be left alone to suck up the best and principalest commodities that the earth there hath given us, what shall become of us, from whom the fruits of our own soil, with the sweat of our brows even up to the knees in mire and dirt, we have laboured for, shall be taken by warrant of supreme authority.

(The last was a mere rhetorical flourish as Martin was no farmer, but a smart London lawyer.) Another lawyer, Francis Moore, said of monopolies:

the end of all is beggary and bondage to the subjects . . . there is no act of hers that hath been or is more derogatory to her own majesty, more odious to the subject, more dangerous to the commonwealth, whilst Lawrence Hyde commented:

as I think it is no derogation to the omnipotence of God to say that he can do all but evil; so I think it is no derogation to the majesty or person of the queen to say the like in some proportion.

Once more the House considered the question of how to proceed. One member noted that the drafting of a bill would touch the prerogative, which, he said sardonically, 'I learnt [in] the last parliament, is so transcendent that the eye of the subject may not aspire thereunto'. Gregory Donhault declared: 'If we proceed by petition we can have no more gracious answer than we had the last parliament to our petitions. Since the parliament we have had no reformation', and Henry Montagu, later earl of Manchester, supported his fellow lawyer Martin, saying, 'I like this matter of proceeding by bill . . . the last parliament we proceeded by way of petition, which had no successful effect'. Three days later the poet John Davies—earlier expelled from the Middle Temple for breaking a cudgel over Martin's head— suggested that they should 'do generously and bravely like parliament-men', that is, 'ourselves send for them and their patents and cancel them before their faces, arraign them as in times past at the bar and send them to the Tower'. Ominously, when the speaker tried to have the subsidy bill read, the House called instead for the monopolies bill. Elizabeth had once more 'to stoop to conquer', with a promise that all burdensome mono- polies would be repealed. Even then, Donhault wanted her reply written in the records, and Davies declared the queen's words 'I think to be gospel; that is glad tidings. And as the gospel is written and registered, so would I have that also'.

A number of grants, including the particularly notorious one for starch, were subsequently cancelled, and subjects were encouraged to try their case against others at common law. James on his accession went further still, issuing a proclamation on 7 May 1603 that suspended all grants except those to corpora- tions and those intended to encourage trade, until their usefulness had been examined by the privy council. But the problem was not yet solved, and in 1604 the debate was widened to take in the monopolies of the great chartered companies, matters which had only occasionally surfaced in the earlier discussions.

Why did monopolies produce so much hostility? There was

clearly very considerable antagonism between those who had
grants and those who did not, some of whom certainly regarded
themselves as more deserving than their favoured colleagues. A
number of those in the House had lucrative grants: Thomas
Knyvet, who sat for Westminster in 1597 and 1601, and Michael
Stanhope, who represented Ipswich in these parliaments, had
both profited from their positions in the privy chamber, for
instance. The patent for the production of ordnance of one
member, Sir Henry Neville, knight for Kent, came under particular attack in 1601; an attempt to induce the House to proceed
by petition and not bill against the patent was then made by Sir
Edward Hoby, whose own patents included one for wool-
buying, and another for half the forfeitures from the prosecutions
of those who through his information were convicted of illegally
exporting iron. Walter Ralegh was said to have 'blushed' in the
parliament of 1601 when the playing-cards monopoly was mentioned; he leapt to his feet later the same day to defend the tin
monopoly, which he also held.

However, it would be an error to see the monopolies debate as
an early example of 'court' and 'country' divisions. Amongst the
harshest critics of monopolies was Gregory Donhault, a servant
of the lord keeper, Thomas Egerton. It was William Cecil's eldest
son, Thomas, who proposed on 8 December 1597 that there
should be 'a bill of petition to her majesty . . . touching monopolies'; meanwhile his half-brother, Robert, was desperately
trying to prevent such a move. Robert Wingfield, a leader of the
attack on monopolies in both 1597 and 1601, was a cousin of
Robert Cecil, to whom he wrote a number of sycophantic letters.
Sir Edward Stanhope, who was very anxious in the parliament of
1601 about the impact of monopolies in his county of Yorkshire,
was the son and brother of the most notorious monopolists of the
period, and also the author of a letter to Robert Cecil asserting
that his appointment as secretary in 1596 'gave great joy to all our
name, who have always depended upon your father and yourself'.

Behind the monopoly debates lurked many private grievances
and disappointments, yet some members clearly felt that the evil
was so great that ties of family and allegiance had to be laid aside.
The source of their concern can easily be discovered. The last two
decades of the sixteenth century, and in particular the 1590s, were
periods of high public expenditure. War with Spain, war with

France, and rebellion in Ireland involved conscription, billeting, and ship money in areas near the coast, as well as purveyance. Parliamentary taxation and forced loans were asked of the whole country. The cost of indirect taxation between 1589 and 1604 has been estimated in one county alone, Kent, as £107,000.[20] This was more than the burden was to be in the 1620s, more, indeed, than at any period before 1640.

This high cost of warfare needs to be set against a background of economic tension. The harvest of 1586/7 was bad, but the early 1590s saw a glut: indeed, moved by 'the great plenty and cheapness of grain', parliament decided in 1593 to repeal the existing statutes against enclosure. From 1594, however, there were four years of bad harvests, and malnutrition combined with bubonic plague produced a demographic downfall. Members of the Commons were sensitive to the changing economic circumstances, as their discussions in 1597 and 1601 make clear: if they had failed to notice before, then the bread riots in London in 1596 and 1597, and the risings or planned risings in Oxfordshire, Norfolk, Somerset, and the North, brought the problem of high prices and poverty to their attention. It is in the context of their anxieties about the economy that we must place members' hostility to monopolies.

At the very least, they realized that monopolies increased still further already high prices: for instance, Edward Stanhope pointed out in 1601 that salt, which had previously cost 16*d.* a bushel, now cost 14*s.* In the same parliament the great critic of monopolies, Robert Wroth, read a list of the patents granted since 1597, which included such important daily items as vinegar, sea-coal, brushes, pots, lead, and oil; this list prompted William Hakewell to demand ironically, 'Is not bread there?' To add to the burdens of an already groaning lower class was regarded as politically unwise, and likely to produce further unrest.

For the Commons, the constitutional issue was also, of course, a central one, a fact which explains the prominent part played by lawyers in the debate. Members knew well by the end of Elizabeth's reign how high a view she took of her prerogative, and all recognized what Dr Bennet said in 1601: 'he that will go about to debate her majesty's prerogative royal had need to walk warily'.

Despite the danger of the queen's wrath, some members were

willing to tangle with the prerogative and attempt to legislate. This desire was stronger in 1601 than it had been in 1597, for members felt that they had been fobbed off with the queen's earlier promise of reform, only to find that 'the grief is still bleeding'. (It is of interest that almost half of those who sat in the Commons in 1601 had also been present in 1597.) However, many of those who were bitterly opposed to monopolies yet thought it pointless to proceed by bill. William Spicer of Warwick, who on 20 November had declared that his town was 'pestered and constantly vexed with the substitutes or vice-regents of these monopolitans', argued on 23 November that the House should merely petition the queen for remedy, since 'it is to no purpose to offer to tie her majesty's hands by way of act of parliament, when she may loose herself at her pleasure'. George More of Loseley took a similar line: 'we know', he said, 'that the power of her majesty cannot be restrained by any act . . . Admit we should make this statute with a non obstante, yet the queen may grant a patent with a non obstante to cross this non obstante'.

The frustration felt by some members is very evident, and there are moments when the debates foreshadow those of the later 1620s. Yet in 1601 the Commons allowed themselves once more to be fobbed off with the queen's promise of reform, despite the unhappy experience of 1597. Indeed, the majority of the House seems to have accepted Elizabeth's message with alacrity, George More declaring, for instance, 'the greater the grievance is and hath been, the more inestimable is the grace of her majesty in repealing them'. Both the scale of the grievance itself, and Elizabeth's elevated view of her prerogative, had led to some extremely difficult moments. None the less, even those who, like Wingfield, were rueful about earlier encounters 'with the word prerogative', were anxious to stress their 'humility'. Although the debates in 1597 and 1601 are marked by frustration and frank speaking, they are also marked by an obvious desire on the part of all those involved to find a compromise, to discover a procedure that would leave no one defeated. In this, most important, way they are different from those of the later 1620s.

7

Conclusion

Parliaments existed to make laws. This function they carried out with remarkable consistency throughout the Tudor period: in Henry VII's reign an average of 27 statutes were passed in each session. The average rose to 44 in the second part of Henry VIII's reign, with a peak in the session of 1540, which saw 80 statutes passed. Under Edward and Mary the average number of statutes passed per session was 27, and in Elizabeth's reign it was 31.

These figures conceal, however, a growth in the number of bills being considered by either or both Houses. No figures can be calculated before 1547 and the beginning of the Commons Journal, and the difficulty of identifying bills even after that makes any precise figures impossible, but the general trend is none the less obvious. Between 1547 and 1558, about 68 bills, on average, were considered in each session. In the first part of Elizabeth's reign, the average was 126, and it was just over 95 in the years after 1584.

The amount of business before parliament was thus much greater under Elizabeth than it had been in the reigns of her brother and sister. However, the length of sessions did not show any corresponding increase. Under Elizabeth the average session lasted less than ten weeks. The shortest Elizabethan session, that of 1576, consisted of just thirty-one working days, yet in that time the Commons considered over a hundred bills. Both Houses therefore found themselves forced to extend their hours of meeting: most of the sessions of the 1570s and 1590s saw the Commons sitting in the afternoon, for example. Both Lords and Commons also tried to distinguish more clearly between important and insignificant proposals: in 1571, for instance, in response to pressure from the Upper House, the Commons set up a committee to decide which bills should be 'first preferred'.

Despite such efforts many bills failed because there was not time to complete all necessary readings, or because there was no opportunity to iron out the problems they raised. In the early part of Elizabeth's reign four-fifths of the bills originating in the Commons failed, and one-third of those in the Lords.[1] Later the Commons were able to secure the enactment of one-third of the bills first presented to them, and the Lords a half. Of course there were many other reasons besides lack of time for a bill's failure, but when it is remembered that besides the bills we can identify there were many others which never got as far as a first reading and are therefore not recorded in the figures, it becomes clear that parliament was not fulfilling the expectations of some of those who looked to it.

Some light is thrown on this failure by an examination of the different 'success' rate of the two Houses, for the Lords clearly coped better with the business before them than did the Commons. They had fewer bills to read, and were therefore able to give more attention to each: in the first part of Elizabeth's reign, for example, only one-quarter of the 885 bills considered originated in the Lords. One hundred and five bills were initiated in the Lords between 1584 and 1601, whereas 468 bills were started in the Commons. Secondly, the Lords had legal assistants —judges and others—to carry out some of the detailed examination of contentious legal points which might otherwise have tied up the Chamber. Thirdly, their procedure was formalized before that of the Commons, which meant that less time was spent considering how to proceed.

Procedure was, of course, becoming more formalized and systematic in the Commons too. The number of readings for a bill had stabilized at three, for example, although occasionally bills were read more often. But there still remained a number of unresolved questions. One that took up some time in 1601 was the problem of whether members who had spoken against a bill could serve on the committee that gave it further consideration: the House eventually voted formally that they could not, but in an amendment to that vote agreed that since the bill under consideration particularly concerned the City of London its representatives could, exceptionally, afforce the committee with their expertise.

Committees were one of the answers to the problem of ever-expanding business, and the use of committees became much more frequent in both Houses in the course of Elizabeth's reign. Committees were also entrusted with more complicated tasks, such as the merging into one of several proposals on the same topic, or the drafting of specific proposals to deal with the generalized worries expressed by members: in 1593, for example, a committee of the Commons was set up to examine the laws relating to the poor. In 1571, when there was considerable pressure of business, a committee was set up to consider 'motions of griefs and petitions' in general, and in 1576 the speaker, Robert Bell, even asked that 'upon every motion made, certain might be appointed to consider whether the matter moved be fit to be committed before any argument should be used of the matter', although in the event nothing seems to have come of this.

The advantages of committees are obvious. They sat before and after the daily session, and thus enabled more work to be got through, they could summon interested parties—Lords' committees very frequently did this—and they could call upon technical expertise. They were chaired by someone other than the speaker, and could thus meet in his absence or illness. Meetings took place in a variety of locations—Commons committees met in the Middle Temple, the Star Chamber, Guildhall, Serjeants' Inn, and members' houses, and Lords committees in the Painted Chamber or the council chamber at Whitehall, or in peers' lodgings, where tables and, sometimes, refreshments, were available. Theoretically, at least, procedure was less formal than in the Chamber, and speeches less rhetorical; however, the comment of one committee man in 1601—'let us . . . leave our orations and speeches, fitter for a parliament than a committee'— suggests that some members did not alter their habits.

Some of these advantages were lost by the increasing tendency of both Houses to create very large committees. In 1589 the committee on the purveyors bill was so big that it had to sit in the Chamber, and the committees set up to consider the subsidy in 1593 and that for laws relating to the poor were both very large— the last consisted of all the councillors and serjeants in the House, as well as sixty named members. Although 'the committee of the whole House' did not formally emerge until the session of 1606–7, the difference between it and some of the committees of the late Elizabethan period is entirely technical.

Because these large committees which needed the Chamber itself to house them look so cumbersome, historians have asked what their purpose was, and have found it in the removal from his chair of the speaker. The speaker was, as we have seen, a crown nominee, and he usually had a close relationship with the privy councillors in the House, who sat on the benches next to him. Frequently they whispered in his ear, and told him which bills they wished to see expedited: in 1572, for instance, when the government wanted the bill against Mary, Queen of Scots, hurried through, one of the councillors, Sir Christopher Hatton, came into the House and spoke quietly to the speaker, who then urged that the first bill read should be that one. As well as deciding the order in which bills were read, the speaker decided when a vote should be taken, and he could so arrange the timing as to favour the government: this is how the first-fruits bill was secured in 1555, and how, according to D'Ewes, the 1593 subsidy bill was expedited. (Not until 1621 did the House decide that a day's notice should be given before the final reading of a bill.)

This kind of manœuvring seems, however, to have been accepted by the House. As we have seen, Anthony Cope complained in 1581 about the speaker joining in debates without the House's permission, and Wentworth's famous questions of 1587 included one on whether 'the speaker may rise when he will, any matter being propounded, without consent of the House', but in general there was little criticism of the relationship between speaker and government. Speakers themselves seem to have operated within certain conventions, as is suggested by a letter to Robert Cecil from the speaker in 1597, apologizing for his failure to secure the passage of a bill favoured by the government. The speaker, Yelverton, told Cecil that he had asked the House whether the bill should be committed, but had received a negative answer. He had suggested engrossment, which had also been refused. He could do no more, Yelverton reported: 'I did favour it as much as, with the dignity of my place, I could.'

Although speakers in the sixteenth century did their best to work with the monarch and council—it was, after all, their function to be a channel of communication between Commons and crown—they showed a surprising spirit of independence at various moments of crisis, the most notable of which was the Commons' address to Mary in 1553 begging her not to marry a foreigner. Good relations between the monarch and the Commons depended from time to time on the tact of the speaker, on his ability to explain the motives of one to the other, and on his willingness to gloss and smooth over unfortunately worded messages. Without some such mediator, relations would have been more difficult.

None the less, as Yelverton's letter to Cecil indicates, the House could and did overrule the speaker when it so wished. It frequently asserted its own choice of priorities in the reading of bills, and the order of business. It is therefore difficult to believe that the committee of the whole House was invented simply as a device for removing from the chair an official who always saw himself as the Commons' servant, not its master.

The explanation for the growth of the committee of the whole House must lie elsewhere. It has to be remembered that in the period before the introduction of a deputy speaker, the House of Commons could be seriously incommoded by the speaker's sickness. In 1584, for example, the government itself was in despair because the subsidy bill 'was like to be hindered, for that the speaker was absent this day by reason of sickness, and so this day lost. And if he should not speedily recover the delay would be greater.' (It is worth noting that when the 'committee of the whole House' emerged under that name for the first time in 1607, it did so because members wanted to go on discussing the bill of hostile laws, but the speaker could not be present.) A committee, however large and cumbersome, eased the life of an otherwise hard-pressed official.

Such committees did not, however, reduce the work-load of the councillors. Because of their superior knowledge and political expertise, councillors were always included in committees. (There was also another, less weighty, reason why they were always nominated: the clerk, in the listing of committees, wrote down 'the names of everyone so called upon, at least wise of such whose names in that confusion he [could] distinctly hear', and the names of councillors would, of course, be well known to him.) On committees, the councillors dominated. A major feature of committees, unlike debates, was that members were allowed to speak more than once to a bill, so that, as Sir Herbert Croft ruefully put it, 'some special persons of place by speaking often and [by] countenance do prevail more than by their reasons'.

The government liked committees, for they promised efficiency. Councillors were always worried about the slow progress of bills in the Commons. In 1571, 1576, and 1581, for instance,

Burghley, by now in the Lords, secured lists of bills still pending
in the Lower House, presumably in order to decide which should
be urged along; perhaps as a result of his interventions, progress
was thereafter a little faster. It was Burghley's son, Robert Cecil,
who impatiently commented in 1601, 'I wish we would not
trouble ourselves with any fantastic speeches or idle bills', and it
was he who proposed in the same parliament that committees
should meet in the afternoon to speed things up. However, the
Commons remained difficult to organize. Even committees did
not always fulfil their purpose. 'Attendance was poor, proceedings inadequate, and often no agreement was reached', one
historian has written of committees in the second part of
Elizabeth's reign.[2] In March 1585, for instance, the attorney of
the court of wards reported that he had attended for a committee
on apprentices in the city of London, but no one else had turned
up. In 1601 Henry Doyle twice came to the place appointed for a
meeting but failed to find his colleagues. Lords' committees
encountered the same problems: in February 1589, for example,
it was reported that they could 'get no meeting but of so small a
number as their Lordships would not deal in it'. Clearly members
of both Houses often found better things to do than attend such
meetings—as someone put it in 1601, 'you call upon men to have
them committees. You think to please them, but they can give
you no thanks for your labour, for they are unwilling.'

Even when the committee members turned up, little might be
done. In his report of a committee meeting in 1584, for instance,
William Fleetwood said that 'twenty at once did speak, and there
we sat talking and did nothing until night'. The Commons was
told in 1593 that the committee considering poor relief 'could
come to no conclusion, but rather to a mere confusion upon the
points of the matter'. Although bills once committed stood,
statistically, a good chance of succeeding, nearly one-quarter of
the bills failing in their house of origin in Elizabeth's later
parliaments did so because they had never emerged from their
committees.

But if committees did not entirely solve the problem of pressure of business in the Commons, they did perhaps create a gap of
interests and even sympathy between the 'good' House of
Commons man, who attended regularly and served on a handful
of committees, and the inexperienced and sometimes rather

uninterested backwoodsmen. It looks as if members sat on increased numbers of committees as their parliamentary experience grew: Sir Henry Gates, for example, sat on only one committee in 1559 and 1563, but on four in 1572, ten in 1576, and seven in 1581. Clearly, some members were recognized as sound committee fodder: Thomas Digges, member for Wallingford, was in 1576 on committees for ports, private bills, unlawful weapons, grants by the dean and chapter of Norwich, salt marshes, benefit of clergy, and excess of apparel. By the 1570s, it appears that the House of Commons felt committees to be incomplete without William Fleetwood, or Thomas Norton, who in 1572 was named to 4 of the recorded 20 bill committees, in 1576 to 22 out of 40, and in 1581 to 27 out of 51. All this was very time-consuming, since many committees met more than once, and members found themselves attending committees before the House met in the morning, in the recess, and even on a Sunday. A gulf was bound to exist between men occupied in this way and those who had sought election primarily in order 'to see fashions'. As a discourse of 1581 explaining how to secure short parliaments noted, new members 'are commonly . . . gladdest of long parliaments to learn and see fashions, where the old continuers have among other things learned more advisedness'. The many complaints recorded in the later part of the sixteenth century about members' time-wasting habits and general inefficiency were usually voiced by the experienced committeemen, and they suggest that the House was becoming divided between the semi-professional 'men of business' and the amateurs.

Naturally, councillors became well acquainted with these semi-professionals, whom they regularly encountered in the House and at committees: it was to them, therefore, that Cecil or Leicester or Hatton would turn when they wished to urge on the queen's business in the House. Committees thus served to strengthen the links between the court and the Commons, but to divide the House itself.

It is clear that more and more Englishmen were looking to parliament to amend what they considered to be abuses. In particular, as the figures show, they looked to the House of

Commons. What was the impact of this heightened interest on the House itself?

Members came to make extensive and solemn claims about the importance of their task: in 1571, for instance, in the debate over Strickland's sequestration, it was asserted that Strickland's absence was dangerous because 'he was not now a private man, but to supply the room, person and place of a multitude, specially chosen and therefore sent'. In 1576 Peter Wentworth echoed these words in his Star Chamber speech, arguing that 'I am now no private person, I am a public, and a councillor to the whole state in that place, where it is lawful for me to speak my mind freely'.

Did sixteenth-century members of the Commons take their task and themselves more seriously than their predecessors had done a century earlier? Those who sat in parliament in the fifteenth century seem, after all, to have had a fairly high notion of their own responsibility: it was Margaret Paston in 1460 who claimed in a letter to her husband, a knight of the shire, that 'you have many good prayers of the poor people that God shall speed you in this parliament, for they live in hope that you shall help to set a way that they might live in better peace'.

The nature of the sources makes answering this question very difficult. There is more evidence available about almost every facet of later sixteenth-century life than there is for earlier periods, and parliament is no exception: as well as the Commons Journal there are numerous speeches, and a number of diaries (no diary exists for any parliament before Elizabeth's reign). Although this growth of interest in the recording of events in the Commons is in itself significant, it obviously reflects changing literary habits as well as changing parliamentary ones. There is, then, for a variety of reasons, a great deal of evidence from the reign of Elizabeth about how members saw their responsibilities, and we have to be very careful not to mistake a greater amount of evidence about members' sense of responsibility for a growth in the thing itself.

Moreover, as a result of the educational changes of the period, members became more anxious to talk about themselves and their solemn responsibilities. Increasingly, sixteenth-century members had been to a university, or to an inn of court. By 1601, almost half the House was university-educated, and more than a half had been admitted to an inn of court. But education, and classical learning, had its negative side: members were all too often anxious to show off. The kind of tortuous speech that resulted, full of allusions to the classics, to mythological figures, and to the more obscure fathers of the church, can be observed in the comments on the 1571 religious bill of the burgess for Warwick, Edward Aglionby, who moved that:

> the law be without exception or privilege for any gentlemen in their private oratories: this did he prove to be fit out of Plato, his laws, and Cicero, both prescribing for the observations of the law an equality between the prince and the poor man . . . also he remembered the authority of Lactantius Firmianus [Christian apologist under Diocletian, 'the Christian Cicero'] . . . the authority of doctors, which he vouched without quoting the place or sentence . . . opinions of fathers and learned men of this land . . . bonae leges ex malis moribus proveniunt.

(Aglionby was not a lawyer, but he was a university man, getting his first degree at Cambridge and then being incorporated at Oxford.) That same year the speaker begged members 'to spend little time on motions, and to avoid long speeches'; his successor a decade later urged members not to speak on the first reading of a bill, and requested that they should avoid 'unnecessary motion and superfluous arguments'. These pleas were not heeded, for rhetoric was a skill much prized in these parliaments. In 1597 Yelverton contrasted speeches in the law courts with those in the Commons: 'there sufficeth plain utterance', he said, 'here it must be accompanied with exact eloquence; there, sound and naked reason is but sought to be delivered; and here, reason must be clothed with elegant speeches'.

It is difficult to distinguish rhetoric about responsibility from a real growth in members' sense of responsibility. In any case, we must differentiate between this generalized sense of responsibility and a feeling of 'accountability' towards a particular constituency. Did members at this period have such a feeling of 'accountability'? Did members, many of whom were not resident in their constituencies, feel any particular obligation towards the people whom they, technically, represented?

It has certainly been argued, most notably by Derek Hirst,[3] that in the early seventeenth century members of the Commons came to feel a new sense of responsibility towards their electorate, to whom they now considered themselves 'accountable':

although members were still elected by a tiny proportion of the population, Hirst suggested that they had come to regard themselves as 'representing' their constituencies in a much wider sense than before, and that they saw themselves as a conduit through which the complaints of their locality could be expressed. Did members in the late sixteenth century consider themselves similarly 'accountable' to their constituents?

Members did, certainly, sometimes describe themselves as 'accountable' to those who had sent them, but usually in the context of taxation. In 1593, for example, one member noted that 'there is no knight of any shire here but representeth many thousands . . . we are stewards of many purses'. Here, what was being expressed was simply the fact that members of the Commons, by assenting to taxation, bound their constituents to its payment. Members' understandable reluctance about returning to tell their friends and neighbours that they had committed them to fairly substantial taxation is a sufficient explanation for this relatively common assertion of responsibility. It should be understood as a weapon in the armoury of tax negotiation rather than an illustration of some new concept of 'accountability'.

Moreover, when members claimed to be speaking for their county or community they may have been doing so in a much looser way than some historians have suggested. For instance, in a debate on the subsidy in 1593, Sir George Carey, knight of the shire for Hampshire, discussed the statement that 'we must regard them and their estates for whom we be here', and said that 'he regarded them and came from them as was meet'. This was mere rhetoric, for few people can have been more autocratic than Carey, a kinsman of the queen. When, as governor of the Isle of Wight, Carey secured the enfranchisement of three boroughs on the island his purpose in so doing was certainly not to enlarge the 'political nation', nor to increase true 'representation'. All three were decayed boroughs, into which Carey could put his own clients: thus, in 1601 blank returns were sent to Carey after he had written to Newtown reminding the borough that as he was 'the means and procurer of the liberty for your corporation' the authorities should 'assemble yourselves together and with your united consent send up to me (as heretofore you have done) your writ, with a blank, wherein I may insert the names of such persons as I shall think fittest to discharge that duty for your behalf'. In 1593 Carey was not expressing any theory of 'accountability', but merely cloaking his own autocratic temperament in a seemly garment.

There are, then, a number of problems in the path of any attempt to judge from their own speeches the extent to which members in the later sixteenth century felt themselves responsible for and to their constituents, and of any attempt to judge whether that feeling of responsibility was changing. But the real test of whether members of the Commons saw themselves as a channel through which the complaints of their localities could flow is surely their readiness to draw attention in the Chamber to the problems of their constituents. The county of Kent, for instance, bore a very heavy weight of taxation in the 1590s, and witnessed considerable local opposition to purveyance, to the 1595 demand for ship money, and to the forced loan of 1597/8. (The government indeed removed twenty-six Kentish gentlemen from the commission of the peace in 1595.) Yet, despite all these problems, only two or three Kentish members are known to have voiced criticism of royal policy during these years. In Norfolk there was similar resistance to compulsory compounding for purveyance, to ship money, and to demands for coat and conduct money, which produced considerable local tension—in 1601 the lord chief justice felt it necessary to instruct magistrates in Norfolk to ensure that no weapons were worn at the quarter sessions in view of the 'heart burning which at this instance is thought to remain unqualified betwixt divers of the chief men of the county'. Yet Norfolk members do not seem to have been vocal in the Commons about the problems of their shire.

When members drew attention to the problems of their constituents, it was almost always because they themselves shared those problems, or were likely to be affected by them. This is why monopolies were so contentious an issue: almost every member of the Commons had a grant of monopoly, or was aggrieved because he did not, or believed that the impact of monopolies on prices was likely to produce domestic unrest. Very rarely do members appear to have acted as 'mouthpieces' for grievances they did not share.

Of course, borough members were sometimes specifically instructed by the town council that had sent them, and particular interest groups, such as in London the leather industry, and in

York the bakers, might tell their representatives how to handle some specific piece of business, but it is rare in the sixteenth century to find other constituents approaching their member about their problems. In 1604 Nathaniel Bacon, one of the knights for Norfolk, was to find himself petitioned by twenty-five master bakers requiring redress against abuses of the statute of artificers; by the inhabitants of Wells-by-the-Sea, who wanted something done about the decay of their fishing; by a King's Lynn corn merchant who proposed an amendment to the statutes regulating the export of corn; and by the inhabitants of marshland who were petitioning for parliamentary relief against the losses they had sustained 'by the over-flowing of the sea'. It is of course probable that other members also received such petitions, and received them earlier, but it is equally obvious that in Elizabeth's reign the privy council and members of the queen's household were the major recipients of grievances: it was to them that complaints about the slow or corrupt administration of justice would be addressed, for example. When constituents did turn to their representative it was either to request him to use his influence 'during the parliament time', but not necessarily in the Chamber itself, or because they wanted something to be done with the legal security that a statute guaranteed.

The absence of any sixteenth-century concept of 'a good constituency member' is particularly noticeable when we examine elections. In borough seats, as we have seen, the important relationship was usually that between candidate and patron, not that between candidate and electors. Edward Lenton, for example, desperate for a seat in the parliament of 1601, wrote to Robert Cecil, saying:

my name has been given by Sir John Fortescue to the corporation of Wycombe to elect me one of their burgesses, but my lord Windsor, their steward, to whom they were wont to grant the nomination of one, has written for both. Wherefore my humble suit is that you would vouchsafe by your letters to give that corporation some encouragement in electing me, for though my lord Windsor objects in his letters that I am one that doth but follow my lord Norris, in whose business I now am, yet I hope your honour knoweth that I have given myself as a servant to none but you.

In the shires, there was no patron, but the important relationship was that between the various county families who had potential candidates. The electors rarely had any real choice, as is clear from a letter of Lord Montagu to the sheriff of Sussex in 1584: 'I have thought good to signify unto you that both sundry noble- men and gentlemen with myself have thought Mr Robert Sackville and Mr Thomas Shirley most fit [to serve as knights of the shire] . . . I pray you to make my wish and desire known to the freeholders there'.

In the counties there was, as Mark Kishlansky has shown,[4] a persistent search for agreement, and a desire at all costs to avoid conflict. Contested elections were therefore rare: as we have already noted, in the Elizabethan period the vast majority of county elections were uncontested. Only when there arose 'bitter personal or local feuds' would there be a contested county election. Such feuds did occur—in Yorkshire in 1597, for instance, and in Norfolk throughout the last decade of Elizabeth's reign—and the elections were correspondingly hard-fought. However, even here the contest was about status and 'face', and no promises were made to the electors about what any candidate would do in parliament were he to be elected.

Indeed, such promises were unlikely while it was still widely believed that not all voters were equal. This, as Kishlansky has pointed out, was why counted votes were mistrusted: they equated the meanest with the greatest. The 'view', which was preferred, existed primarily not to decide which side had the largest number of voters, but which had the most prestigious: this was where the nobleman's retainers, wearing his colours, would sway the humbler freeholders. Whilst electors remained so profoundly 'unequal', elections would not be a contest for quantity but rather one for quality: only when a quantity of votes was sought would election promises start to come in.

Thus, it seems unlikely that members' relationships with their constituents were much changed by the end of the sixteenth century, or even that members' sense of responsibility in a more generalized sense was increasing.

None the less, it is possible that, for other reasons, members' attitude toward parliament and their own position in the Commons was changing. In the later sixteenth century there is evident, for example, an increased interest and pride in the institution of parliament and in its history, which was probably the result of members' improved education. Thomas Smith, John Hooker, and William Lambarde all wrote extensively in Elizabeth's reign on the history and authority of parliament. The antiquity of their institution was constantly stressed by those in the Commons—and the worst insult Arthur Hall could offer in 1576 after he had been censured by the Commons was to say that 'until the 20th year of Henry III I hear of no parliament, unless you will have all consultations parliaments'. This historical sense was given shape with the foundation by William Camden about 1586 of the Society of Antiquaries, a learned body whose members included a number of those in the Commons, such as Sir Robert Cotton, Robert Beale, Thomas Lake, later secretary of state to James I, James Ley, member for Westbury in 1597 and subsequently chief justice of King's Bench and earl of Marlborough, William Hakewill, and James Whitelocke.

It is probable that their knowledge of and interest in the history of parliament made the Commons more sensitive about their own privileges, which were formalized and extended in the sixteenth century. Ferrers' case of 1542 had confirmed the right of members to freedom from civil suits in time of parliament, whilst Smiley's case of 1576 protected members' servants. Martin's case of 1587 settled the vexed question of how long the privilege should extend before and after a meeting. Moreover—and it is an indication of the Commons' growing self-confidence—the Lower House began to feel that it alone could decide upon such matters: by the time that Thomas Smith wrote in the 1560s the speaker routinely requested at the beginning of a session that 'offences by any of the House may be punishable but by the House' itself. The House did indeed punish its own members: Arthur Hall in 1572, Peter Wentworth in 1576, and Arthur Hall again in 1581. In 1593 it even set up a committee to consider privileges and liberties. (This committee also took on the scrutiny of election returns.) The Commons' self-confidence moved in 1601 into pomposity when Sir Robert Cecil, who had unwisely suggested that the speaker should 'attend' the lord keeper, was reproved and informed that the speaker of the Commons 'is to be commanded by none'.

It is tempting to see in this growing historical awareness something inherently hostile to royal power and control. Christopher Hill, for example, argued that under Charles, Sir

Robert Cotton and Sir Edward Coke 'suffered for saying the
wrong things about the past . . . the parliamentary opposition's
case against the first two Stuarts was wholly based on history,
even if this history was not always very accurate'. Hill wished to
throw all the antiquaries sitting in parliament, and parliament's
growing interest in its own history, into the scales as things
bound to upset the Stuart constitution.[5] However, recent
scholarship has led to a questioning of this link. History, it is
clear, could be appealed to by either side. In 1604, for instance, Sir
Robert Cotton worked on his records in order to prove in
parliament the king's case for union with Scotland, and in 1610 he
pressed the king's request for aid by a reference to Henry IV, but
he also used his skills to assist in the drawing up of a list of
Commons grievances.[6]

Lawyers, like antiquaries, have also been thrown into the
balance against the crown, and the increasingly legally trained
nature of the Commons has been seen as something inherently
disagreeable for the crown. Notestein declared in 1924:

the influence of lawyers upon the new developments in the Commons
can hardly be over-estimated . . . [they] were more than abettors of
opposition to James, they made up a considerable part of the leadership
of that opposition . . . Many a Tudor gentleman, who had never sailed
the Spanish main, or put together a play, had let his imagination run into
law and had caught in the orderliness of complicated legal conceptions
beauty and rhythm, even poetry.[7]

But professional lawyers, at least, were more interested in their
careers than they were in the poetry of the law: Coke is an
obvious example here, as are Hakewill, Whitelocke, and Digges
(master of the rolls). The lawyer and antiquarian William Noy
could indeed be found opposing the crown's proceedings in the
parliament of 1610, and in 1621 he was kept busy looking up
medieval precedents to justify the Commons' attack on monopolies. Noy resisted the granting of tonnage and poundage for
life to Charles I and defended Sir Walter Erle when he was
imprisoned for opposing the forced loan of 1626. But in 1631
Noy became attorney-general, and throughout the 1630s he used
his legal and antiquarian skills to find ways of increasing royal
revenues: he was prominent in the prosecution of Prynne and the
feoffees for impropriations, and in the drawing up of the ship
money writs.

There is no reason to believe that the increased historical and legal awareness of the Commons was in itself inimical to royal authority. It changed the shape taken by debates, of course, which became littered with recondite historical and legal examples, such as that produced in the course of the 1601 monopolies debate by Lawrence Hyde, who declared that one John Peach had been arraigned at the bar of the House in the reign of Edward III for possession of a sweet-wine monopoly. Members of the Commons were perhaps prouder than in the past of their House and its (often invented) history, and they were more self-confident about its procedure, but these changes had no discernible impact in the sixteenth century on their relationships with either the monarch or their constituencies.

It was not, then, primarily changes in the character of composition of the House of Commons that caused tension in Elizabeth's parliaments: rather it was the existence of a number of highly important and controversial problems, many of which the queen wanted to prevent parliament from discussing. In issues of religion, over the question of her marriage and the succession, and where prerogative finance was concerned, Elizabeth, as we have seen, took a quite different line from her predecessors. The fact that earlier parliaments had legislated on matters that they were not now allowed even to discuss did not escape the attention of Elizabeth's critics. In 1601, for instance, when the export of ordnance was being discussed, and the familiar problem arose of whether to proceed by bill or petition, one member pointed out that there had been statutes in the past dealing with the problem, and Lawrence Hyde, a great critic of monopolies, commented ironically:

I see no reason but we may well proceed by bill, and not touch her majesty's prerogative, for her majesty is not more careful and watchful of her prerogative than the noble princes of famous memory King Henry VIII her father and King Edward VI her brother were. Then there was no doubt or mention of the prerogative.

However, the parliaments of Elizabeth's reign never tackled the problem head-on, as their successors were to do in 1624 with the statute of monopolies, 'the first statutory invasion of the prerogative'. In the end, and despite much grumbling, they were willing to accept the queen's promises of reform. Although, then, Elizabeth created an immense problem by her wish to exclude more and more aspects of government from the purview of parliament, the desire of those in parliament for agreement, and their reluctance to speak of the monarch other than with 'reverence', prevented the situation deteriorating still further.

None the less, it cannot be denied that parliament, and in particular the House of Commons, conducted itself in a fairly boisterous manner in the last decade of Elizabeth's reign. In 1601, for example, two members stood up to speak at the same time, and neither would yield to the other; there was a great commotion, and the comptroller of the queen's household declared himself 'sorry to see this confusion in the House; it were better we used more silence, and kept better order'. Earlier, in the course of the monopolies debate, Robert Cecil had commented:

I have been . . . a member of this House in six or seven parliaments, yet never did I see the House in so great confusion. I believe there never was in any parliament a more tender point handled than the liberty of the subject, that when any is discussing this point, he should be cried and coughed down. This is more fit for a grammar school than a court of parliament.

A boisterous House was more difficult for the speaker and the council to manage than a well-conducted one. In 1601 Mr Carey asserted, in the middle of a dispute over the order in which bills were to be read, that 'in the Roman senate, the consul always appointed what should be read, what not: so may our speaker, whose place is a consul's'. At this, some members hissed, and Mr Wiseman declared, 'ours is a municipal government, and we know our own grievances better than Mr Speaker'.

However, it is important not to make too much of such scenes, nor to use them to postulate a steady growth of opposition to the crown in these later parliaments. Much has been made of the fact that in 1593 the queen found it necessary to tell the Commons that she 'misliked . . . such irreverence [as] was showed towards privy councillors', but it is worth noticing that in her differentiation between privy councillors and 'common knights and burgesses of the House, that are councillors but during the parliament', Elizabeth was in fact accepting the Commons' high opinion of its own importance. It has also to be remembered that as long ago as 1532 the Commons had 'made use in public of very strong language against the king, his privy council and government' (see above, p. 72).

Despite the boisterousness of Elizabeth's later parliaments, they were in some ways easier for the crown than those of the 1560s, 1570s, and 1580s, when those in the Lower House who wished to settle the succession and further reform the church had been supported by members of Elizabeth's own council, such as Mildmay and Walsingham. The real defeats for Elizabeth in parliament had come in 1559, when she was forced to accept a more radical religious settlement than she wanted, and in 1566 when to avoid discussion of the succession she gave up a part of the subsidy. The outcome of the monopolies debates of 1597 and 1601 was, by contrast, entirely favourable to the queen, for the House of Commons then confined itself to petitioning about reform, thus leaving the prerogative 'transcendent'.

This fact has been obscured by historians' over-concentration on 'management', and in particular the role of the privy councillors.[8] It was, of course, a very important development for the Commons when councillors came to seek election there: whereas very few of Henry VII's councillors sat in the Commons—Sir Reginald Bray, Sir Thomas Lovell—by the time of Edward VI's first parliament nine privy councillors had found seats. In 1553 the council took some considerable pains to find councillors seats in Edward's second parliament. In each of Mary's parliaments between ten and eighteen councillors had seats. The number dropped under Elizabeth, who had a smaller council, but almost all who did not have a place in the Lords sought a seat in the Commons. The number of councillors sitting in the House then diminished markedly in the early Stuart period: there were only two in 1604, which was the reason why the government tried to job in Fortescue, and only four in 1614. Not until 1621, when nine councillors sat in the Commons, did numbers reach anything like the Tudor average. This drop has led some historians to attribute James's difficulties in parliament to an absence of management, just as the greater obstreperousness of the Commons in the 1590s could be attributed to a decline in the number of councillors there, partly because of the deaths of 'old hands' such as Knollys and Mildmay, and partly as a result of Elizabeth's desire to keep down the size of the privy council.

Certainly a conciliar presence in the Commons was of considerable significance. Pollard long ago noted that the decision of members of the council to submit to election and to sit in the Commons was of vital importance, for 'if parliament was to remain something more than an irresponsible opposition, there must be unity between it and the government'.[9] One task of the council in the Commons was, like that of the speaker, to create such unity by explaining the intentions of the monarch to the House, and vice versa. This role was particularly important when grants of taxation were under consideration, for the councillors knew the state of royal finances and could set out the problems. But councillors also urged along measures in which the monarch was particularly interested, and suppressed those to which he was opposed. This could be done by gentle means, or by forceful ones. When the 1547 chantries act ran into difficulties (see above, pp. 80–1) it was privy councillors sitting in the House who went to persuade the members for King's Lynn and Coventry 'to desist from further speaking and labouring against the said article'. Sometimes their methods were harsher. According to Peter Wentworth, after Robert Bell had attacked monopolies in 1571, with a 'very good speech for the calling in of certain licences granted to four courtiers to the utter undoing of six or eight thousand of the Queen's Majesty's subjects', he was sent for by some of the council,

and so hardly dealt with that he came [back] into the House with such an amazed countenance that it daunted all the House in such sort that for 10, 12, or 16 days there was not one of the House that durst deal in any matter of importance, and in those simple matters that they dealt in they spent more words and time in their preamble requiring that they might not be [misunderstood] then they did in the matter they spake unto. This inconvenience grew into the House by the councillors' hard handling of the same member.

Councillors did not always need to do anything to secure what they wanted, for their very position commanded respect. As Wentworth bitterly remarked, 'it was common policy in this House to mark the best sort of the same and either to sit or arise [i.e. vote] with them'. The unsophisticated or inexperienced member—and in any parliament up to half the members had not sat before—must often have trimmed his opinions to match those of the councillors, if only because they would be expected to be in full knowledge of the facts.

But privy council control of the Lower House was never complete. If it had been, there would have been no need for the monarch to intervene in person, as Henry VIII did on a number of occasions, and as Mary did in 1555, when she sent for members of both Houses and addressed them 'gravely and piously' after the first-fruits bill had run into difficulties. Another indication of the fact that managerial techniques were never totally successful in the sixteenth century is the royal use of the veto: Henry VII, after all, had never been forced to veto a bill, since no bill he disliked was ever passed by both Houses. Henry VIII found it necessary to veto bills only rarely. But Elizabeth used the veto in every parliament, and twelve times in 1597. This appears to have been acceptable to contemporaries, who regarded the crown as a working part of the trio of king, lords, and commons—and went on so doing until 1708—but it certainly does show that parliament was more than a mere puppet of the council.

In any case, the council had rarely spoken with one voice, or even with the same intentions as the monarch. Under Elizabeth, in particular, it is clear that the council had very different views about the succession, Mary, Queen of Scots, and the state of the church, from those of the queen herself. Privy councils necessarily contained men of differing views whose solutions to problems were also varied. This variety could be fruitful—all solutions to a problem might be discussed and considered before a decision was taken—but it could also produce conflict so serious that the actual working of government was threatened. If this happened in time of parliament, the efficient conduct of crown business might be one of the first things to suffer.

This was obvious, for example, in the middle years of the century. A very clear and dangerous example of conciliar quarrels spilling over into parliament is that of Thomas Seymour. In Mary's reign, conciliar disagreements also caused problems. Lord Paget sought to do down Stephen Gardiner, bishop of Winchester, by crushing his plans for the persecution of heresy when they were introduced into the House of Lords in April 1554. The heresy bill was lost, and a bill extending the protection of the treason laws to Mary's future husband, Philip of Spain, was also badly mauled. Paget's attack on Gardiner, supported as it was by the earl of Pembroke and Lord Rich, closely resembles the attack on Buckingham in 1626 led by the earl of Arundel and a later earl of Pembroke.

Such tactics did not occur again for some years, and privy councillors do not seem to have used parliament so openly in this way in the first decades of Elizabeth's reign, despite often being divided. However, Sir John Neale believed that the spilling over of conciliar faction, which he called 'a leprosy . . . that had infected far and near', began again in the 1590s, with the struggle between the earl of Essex and Robert Cecil.[10] Certainly Cecil in 1597 put about thirty of his clients into the House of Commons, and he even wrote to unenfranchised areas such as Doncaster and the county of Durham in the hope of finding vacant seats there. Whether this is as significant as Neale believed, however, is doubtful. Essex was, after all, in the end defeated by his own foolish behaviour, both in Ireland and subsequently in London, not as a result of manoeuvres in parliament. Moreover, Essex's fall did not stop Cecil being very active in the elections of 1601. He was known to be on the look-out for seats for his clients, thirty of whom were to be returned, for one Jonathan Trelawny then wrote presenting him with 'two burgess-ships for this parliament'. Cecil was clearly interested in parliamentary seats primarily as opportunities for patronage, and that is how most councillors saw them at this time.

Thus, although the possibility of conciliar conflict spilling over into parliament was obviously always there in the sixteenth century, when so many members owed their seats to some magnate or councillor and might in a moment of crisis be required to repay their patrons with their support, the actual instances of it so doing are few. It was to be much more common under the Stuarts, causing the total breakdown of the 1614 parliament, and the fall of Lionel Cranfield in 1624, when the duke of Buckingham used his clients in the House of Commons to destroy his fellow councillor. It is to this spilling over into parliament of conciliar conflict, rather than to any absence of management, that we should attribute the greater difficulties of the Stuarts with their parliaments.

How else can we explain these difficulties? James's decision to increase the number of peers, however justified in general terms, made the House of Lords, once the more efficient and orderly of

the two chambers, factious and unwieldy. In the mid and late
1620s, religious issues also began again to divide those in parliament. However, unlike the 1560s and 1570s, those in parliament
who were critical of the crown's religious policy did not this time
have any councillors other than Bishop Williams to support
them: Buckingham, for instance, had jumped onto the Arminian
bandwagon at the York House conference. Elizabeth doubtless
found the criticisms of her church policy voiced by Mildmay,
Walsingham, and even Burghley, very tiresome, but it prevented
that division between court and country which is sometimes
visible in Stuart parliaments.

But, above all, what went wrong was money. Although
Conrad Russell and the 'revisionists' have suggested that parliament was always willing to grant the crown taxation, the propertied classes were not ready to subsidize the crown through
a myriad of other means, such as feudal dues, monopolies, and
impositions. But the Stuarts had to look to these because the
Tudors had never succeeded in putting the crown's finances on
a strong long-term basis. Instead, they had lived off occasional
windfalls—monastery land, chantries, debasement, bishops'
lands—and rewarded their servants out of the pockets of their
subjects. The crunch was bound to come.

Tudor and Stuart government rested on an alliance between
the crown and the propertied classes, an alliance that was very
evident in parliament. Indeed, a useful way of looking at parliaments in this period is to see them as shareholders' meetings:
meetings of men devoted to the same purposes, although sometimes disagreeing about how best to achieve them. When the
shareholders began to feel that the directors no longer had their
interests primarily at heart, trouble began. In other words, we
cannot explain the parliamentary history of the Tudors and early
Stuarts by looking at parliament alone, nor even parliament and
the court alone: we need to look at the whole range of ties that
bound together the crown and the property-owning classes.

Notes

CHAPTER I

1. J. S. Roskell, 'Perspectives in English Parliamentary History', in E. B. Fryde and E. Miller (eds.), *Historical Studies of the English Parliament*, ii (Cambridge, 1970), 296–323.
2. E. R. Foster, *The House of Lords, 1603–1640* (Chapel Hill, NC, and London, 1983), 186.
3. R. W. K. Hinton, 'The Decline of Parliamentary Government under Elizabeth I and the Early Stuarts', *Cambridge Historical Journal*, 13 (1957), 116–32.
4. F. A. Youngs, *The Proclamations of the Tudor Queens* (Cambridge, 1976), 9.
5. G. R. Elton, 'Henry VIII's Act of Proclamations', *English Historical Review*, 75, (1960), 208–22; J. Hurstfield, *Freedom, Corruption and Government in Elizabethan England* (Cambridge, Mass., 1973), 33–40; R. W. Heinze, *The Proclamations of the Tudor Kings* (Cambridge, 1976), ch. 6; M. L. Bush, 'The Act of Proclamations: A Reinterpretation', *American Journal of Legal History*, 27 (1983), 33–53.
6. R. W. Heinze, 'Proclamations and Parliamentary Protest, 1539–1610', in D. J. Guth and J. W. McKenna (eds.), *Tudor Rule and Revolution* (Cambridge, 1982), 237–59.
7. G. W. Bernard, *War, Taxation and Rebellion in Early Tudor England* (Brighton, 1986), 150–2.

CHAPTER 2

1. M. A. R. Graves, *The House of Lords in the Parliaments of Edward VI and Mary I: An Institutional Study* (Cambridge, 1981), 140.
2. H. Miller, 'Attendance in the House of Lords during the Reign of Henry VIII', *Historical Journal*, 10 (1967), 325–51; V. F. Snow, 'Proctorial Representation and Conciliar Management during the Reign of Henry VIII', *Historical Journal*, 9 (1966), 1–26; idem, 'Proctorial Representation in the House of Lords during the Reign of Edward VI', *Journal of British Studies*, 8 (1969), 1–27; M. A. R. Graves, 'Proctorial Representation in the House of Lords during Edward VI's Reign: A Reassessment', *Journal of British Studies*, 10 (1971), 17–35, and rejoinder by Snow, pp. 36–46.

3. P. W. Hasler (ed.), *The House of Commons, 1558–1603* (London, 1981), i. 40.

4. R. Horox, 'Urban Patronage and Patrons in the Fifteenth Century', in R. Griffiths (ed.), *Patronage, The Crown and The Provinces* (Gloucester, 1981), 158.

5. G. L. Harriss, in his introduction to K. B. McFarlane, *England in the Fifteenth Century* (London, 1981), p. xvii.

6. C. S. L. Davies, *Peace, Print and Protestantism* (London, 1977), 56–7.

7. J. K. Gruenfelder, *Influence in Early Stuart Elections, 1604–1640* (Columbus, Ohio, 1981), 213.

8. G. R. Elton, 'The Points of Contact: Parliament', in idem, *Studies in Tudor and Stuart Politics and Government*, iii (Cambridge, 1983), 16–20.

9. Hasler, *House of Commons*, p. 15.

10. W. J. Jones, *Politics and the Bench* (London, 1971), 46. See also M. A. R. Graves, 'The Common Lawyers and the Privy Council's Parliamentary Men-of-Business, 1584–1601', *Parliamentary History*, 8 (1989), 189–215.

11. G. R. Elton, 'Parliament in the Sixteenth Century: Functions and Fortunes', in idem, *Studies in Tudor and Stuart Politics and Government*, iii. 162.

CHAPTER 3

1. I am very grateful for this information to Miss B. F. Harvey.

2. M. A. R. Graves, *The House of Lords in the Parliaments of Edward VI and Mary I: An Institutional Study* (Cambridge, 1981), 179–82.

3. G. R. Elton, *The Parliament of England, 1559–1581* (Cambridge, 1986), 92–3.

4. M. A. R. Graves, *The Tudor Parliaments: Crown, Lords and Commons, 1485–1603* (London, 1985), 17. In this work Graves retracts his earlier assertion somewhat: see e.g. p. 10.

5. J. G. Edwards, 'The Emergence of Majority Rule in the Procedure of the House of Commons', *Transactions of the Royal Historical Society*, 5th ser., 15 (1965), 165–87.

6. Elton, *Parliament*, pp. 123–5.

CHAPTER 4

1. G. R. Elton, *Reform and Reformation* (London, 1977), 55–6.

2. S. Gunn, 'The Act of Resumption of 1515', in D. T. Williams (ed.), *Early Tudor England*, forthcoming.

3. See e.g. Elton, *Reform and Reformation*, pp. 88–91, and J. Guy, 'Wolsey and the Parliament of 1523', in C. Cross, D. Loades, and J. J. Scarisbrick (eds.), *Law and Government under the Tudors* (Cambridge, 1988), 1–18. R. L. Woods, 'Politics and Precedent: Wolsey's Parliament of 1523', *Huntington Library Quarterly*, 40 (1976–7), 297–312, however, presents a quite different interpretation.

4. G. Bernard, *War, Taxation and Rebellion in Early Tudor England* (Brighton, 1986), 121.

5. Guy, 'Wolsey', pp. 6–18.

6. J. S. Roskell, *The Commons and their Speakers in English Parliaments, 1376–1523* (Manchester, 1965), 43.

7. Ibid. 50.

8. H. Miller, 'London and Parliament in the Reign of Henry VIII', in E. B. Fryde and E. Miller (eds.), *Historical Studies of the English Parliament*, ii (Cambridge, 1970), 140–1.

9. C. A. Haigh, 'Anticlericalism and the English Reformation', *History*, 68 (1983), 396.

10. For a full discussion of the difficult question of the origins of the Supplication, see Elton, *Reform and Reformation*, pp. 150–5, and the references there given.

11. G. R. Elton, 'Taxation for War and Peace in Early-Tudor England', in idem, *Studies in Tudor and Stuart Politics and Government*, iii (Cambridge, 1983), 142–55.

12. G. L. Harriss, 'Thomas Cromwell's "New Principle" of Taxation', *English Historical Review*, 93 (1978), 721–38. See also J. D. Alsop, 'The Theory and Practice of Tudor Taxation', ibid. 97 (1982), 1–30.

CHAPTER 5

1. B. L. Beer, 'A Critique of the Protectorate: An Unpublished Letter of Sir William Paget to the Duke of Somerset', *Huntington Library Quarterly*, 34 (1971), 277–83.

2. J. J. Scarisbrick, *The Reformation and the English People* (Oxford, 1984), 67–8.

3. W. Notestein, *The Winning of the Initiative by the House of Commons* (London, 1924), 11; J. E. Neale, *Elizabeth I and her Parliaments, 1559–1581* (London, 1953), 21–3.

4. J. I. Miklovitch, 'Legislative Procedure in the Reign of Henry VIII, 1536–1547' (unpublished Cambridge Ph.D. thesis, 1974), 156.

5. For a further account of this episode, see J. Loach, *Parliament and the Crown in the Reign of Mary Tudor* (Oxford, 1986), 45–50, 119–22, and appendix A.

6. M. A. R. Graves, *The House of Lords in the Parliaments of Edward VI and Mary I: An Institutional Study* (Cambridge, 1981), 196–8.

CHAPTER 6

1. W. P. Haugaard, *Elizabeth and the English Reformation* (Cambridge, 1968), 82.

2. *The Cambridge Connection and the Elizabethan Settlement of 1559* (Durham, NC, 1980).

3. *Faith by Statute* (London, 1982).

4. The 'black rubric', so called because it was printed in black-letter type, was a note added to the 1552 Prayer Book at the insistence of John Knox, explaining that kneeling to receive the sacrament did not imply adoration.

5. Jones, *Faith by Statute*, ch. 7; G. Alexander, 'Bishop Bonner and the Parliament of 1559', *Bulletin of the Institute of Historical Research*, 56 (1983), 164–79.

6. J. E. Neale, *Elizabeth I and her Parliaments, 1559–1581* (London, 1953), 91–2.

7. G. R. Elton, *The Parliament of England, 1559–1581* (Cambridge, 1986), 351–4.

8. M. A. R. Graves, 'Thomas Norton the Parliament Man: An Elizabethan MP, 1559–1581', *Historical Journal*, 23 (1980), 17–35. See also, however, P. Collinson, 'Puritans, Men of Business and Elizabethan Parliaments', *Parliamentary History*, 7 (1988), 187–211.

9. D. Hirst, *The Representative of the People?* (Cambridge, 1975), 210–12.

10. P. Hughes, *The Reformation in England* (London, 1963), iii. 362.

11. Elton, *Parliament*, pp. 263–7.

12. Joan Kent, 'Attitudes of Members of the House of Commons to the Regulation of "Personal Conduct" in Late Elizabethan and Early Stuart England', *Bulletin of the Institute of Historical Research*, 46 (1973), 41–71.

13. I. Archer, 'The London Lobbies in the Later Sixteenth Century', *Historical Journal*, 31 (1988), 17–44.

14. Idem, in an unpublished paper, 'The Armourers' Lobby in 1581'. I am very grateful to Mr Archer for a copy of this paper.

15. D. M. Dean, 'Public or Private? London, Leather and Legislation in Elizabethan England', *Historical Journal*, 31 (1988), 525–48.

16. Neale, *Elizabeth I*, p. 133.

17. J. D. Alsop, 'Innovation in Tudor Taxation', *English Historical Review*, 99 (1984), 83–93.

18. For a different interpretation, see Elton, *Parliament*, pp. 364–74.

19. A. Hassell Smith, *County and Court: Government and Politics in Norfolk, 1558–1603* (Oxford, 1974), 246.

20. P. Clark, *English Provincial Society from the Reformation to the Revolution: Religion, Politics and Society in Kent, 1500–1640* (Hassocks, 1977), 228.

CHAPTER 7

1. The figures for the first part of the reign are taken from G. R. Elton, *The Parliament of England, 1559–1581* (Cambridge, 1986), and those for the second part from D. M. Dean, 'Bills and Acts, 1584–1601' (unpublished Cambridge Ph.D. thesis, 1984).

2. Dean, 'Bills and Acts', p. 253.

3. *The Representative of the People?* (Cambridge, 1975).

4. *Parliamentary Selection* (Cambridge, 1986).

5. *Intellectual Origins of the Civil War* (Oxford, 1965).

6. K. Sharpe, *Sir Robert Cotton, 1586–1631* (Oxford, 1979), 152, 160.

7. W. Notestein, *The Winning of the Initiative by the House of Commons* (London, 1924), 49–51.

8. See e.g. D. H. Willson, *The Privy Councillors in the House of Commons, 1604–1629* (Minneapolis, 1940).

9. A. F. Pollard, *The Evolution of Parliament* (London, 1926), 297.

10. J. E. Neale, *The Elizabethan House of Commons* (London, 1949), ch. 11.

Additional Reading

CHAPTER 1

DAVIES, R. G., and DENTON, J. H. (eds.), *The English Parliament in the Middle Ages* (Manchester, 1981).

HARRISS, G. L., *King, Parliament and Public Finance in Mediaeval England to 1369* (Oxford, 1975).

ROSKELL, J. S., *The Commons and their Speakers in English Parliaments, 1376–1523* (Manchester, 1965).

RUSSELL, C., 'Parliamentary History in Perspective', *History*, 61 (1976), 1–27.

CHAPTER 2

EDWARDS, J. G., 'The Emergence of Majority Rule in English Parliamentary Elections', *Transactions of the Royal Historical Society*, 5th ser., 14 (1964), 175–96.

HAWKYARD, A. D. K., 'The Wages of Members of Parliament, 1509–1558', *Parliamentary History*, 6 (1987), 302–11.

KEELER, M. F., 'The Emergence of Standing Committees for Privileges and Returns', *Parliamentary History*, 1 (1982), 25–46.

LOACH, J., 'Parliament: A New Air?', in C. Coleman and D. Starkey (eds.), *Revolution Reassessed* (Oxford, 1986), 117–34.

McKISACK, M., *The Parliamentary Representation of English Boroughs during the Middle Ages* (Oxford, 1932).

NEALE, J. E., *The Elizabethan House of Commons* (London, 1949).

CHAPTER 3

ELTON, G. R., 'The Sessional Printing of Statutes, 1484–1547', in idem, *Studies in Tudor and Stuart Politics and Government*, iii (Cambridge, 1983), 92–109.

MILLER, H., 'Lords and Commons: Relations between the Two Houses of Parliament, 1509–1558', *Parliamentary History*, 1 (1982), 13–24.

CHAPTER 4

BEAN, J. M. W., *The Decline of English Feudalism, 1215–1540* (London, 1968).

BELLAMY, J. G., *Criminal Law and Society in late Mediaeval and Tudor England* (Gloucester and New York, 1984), ch. 5.

Additional Reading 167

CHRIMES, S. B., *Henry VII* (London, 1972).
ELTON, G. R., 'The Evolution of a Reformation Statute', in idem, *Studies in Tudor and Stuart Politics and Government*, ii (Cambridge, 1974), 82–106.
IVES, E. W., 'The Genesis of the Statute of Uses', *English Historical Review*, 82 (1967), 673–97.
LANDER, J. R., 'Attainder and Forfeiture, 1453–1509', *Historical Journal*, 4 (1961), 119–51.
LEHMBERG, S. E., *The Reformation Parliament, 1529–1536* (Cambridge, 1970).
SCARISBRICK, J. J., 'Fisher, Henry VIII and the Reformation Crisis', in B. Bradshaw and E. Duffy (eds.), *Humanism, Reform and the Reformation: The Career of Bishop John Fisher* (Cambridge, 1989, 155–68.

CHAPTER 5

DAVIES, C. S. L., 'Slavery and Protector Somerset: The Vagrancy Act of 1547', *Economic History Review*, 2nd ser., 19 (1966), 533–49.
KREIDER, A., *English Chantries: The Road to Dissolution* (Cambridge, Mass., and London, 1979), ch. 8.
LEHMBERG, S. E., *The Later Parliaments of Henry VIII, 1536–1547* (Cambridge, 1977).
REDWORTH, G., 'A Study in the Formulation of Policy: The Genesis and Evolution of the Act of Six Articles', *Journal of Ecclesiastical History*, 37 (1986), 42–67.
STACY, W. R., 'Richard Roose and the Use of Parliamentary Attainder in the Reign of Henry VIII', *Historical Journal*, 29 (1986), 1–39.

CHAPTER 6

ALSOP, J. D., 'The Theory and Practice of Tudor Taxation', *English Historical Review*, 97 (1982), 1–30.
BARTLETT, K. R., 'The Role of the Marian Exiles', appendix XI in P. W. Hasler (ed.), *The House of Commons, 1558–1603*, i (London, 1981), 102–10.
BELL, H. E., *An Introduction to the History and Records of the Court of Wards and Livery* (Cambridge, 1953).
CROFT, P., 'Free Trade and the House of Commons, 1605–6', *Economic History Review*, 2nd ser., 28 (1975), 17–27; 'Wardship in the Parliament of 1604', *Parliamentary History*, 2 (1983), 39–48; 'Parliament, Purveyance and the City of London, 1589–1608', ibid. 5 (1985), 9–34. See also E. Linquist, 'The Bills against Purveyors', ibid. 35–43.
DEAN, D., 'London Lobbies and Parliament: The Case of the Brewers and Coopers in the Parliament of 1593', *Parliamentary History*, 8 (1989), 341–65.

DIETZ, F. C., *English Public Finance, 1558–1641* (New York and London, 1932).

GRAVES, M. A. R., 'The Management of the Elizabethan House of Commons: The Council's Men of Business', *Parliamentary History*, 2 (1983), 11–38.

HEAL, F., 'Clerical Tax Collection under the Tudors', in R. O'Day and F. Heal (eds.), *Continuity and Change* (Leicester, 1976), 97–122.

PRICE, W. H., *The English Patents of Monopoly* (Boston, Mass., 1906).

RABB, T. K., 'Free Trade and the Gentry in the Parliament of 1604', *Past and Present*, 40 (1968), 165–73.

SCHOFIELD, R., 'Taxation and the Political Limits of the Tudor State', in C. Cross, D. M. Loades, and J. J. Scarisbrick (eds.), *Law and Government under the Tudors* (Cambridge, 1988), 227–56.

SLACK, P. A., *Poverty and Policy in Tudor and Stuart England* (London, 1988), ch. 6.

WOLFFE, B. P., *The Royal Demense in English History* (London, 1971).

WOODWARD, A., *Purveyance for the Royal Household in the Reign of Elizabeth* (Philadelphia, 1945).

CHAPTER 7

FOSTER, E. R., *The House of Lords, 1603–1649* (Chapel Hill, NC, and London, 1983).

JONES, W. J., *Politics and the Bench* (London, 1971).

LAMBERT, S., 'Procedure in the House of Commons in the Early Stuart Period', *English Historical Review*, 95 (1980), 753–81.

RUSSELL, C., 'Parliament and the King's Finances', in C. Russell (ed.), *The Origins of the English Civil War* (London, 1973).

Index